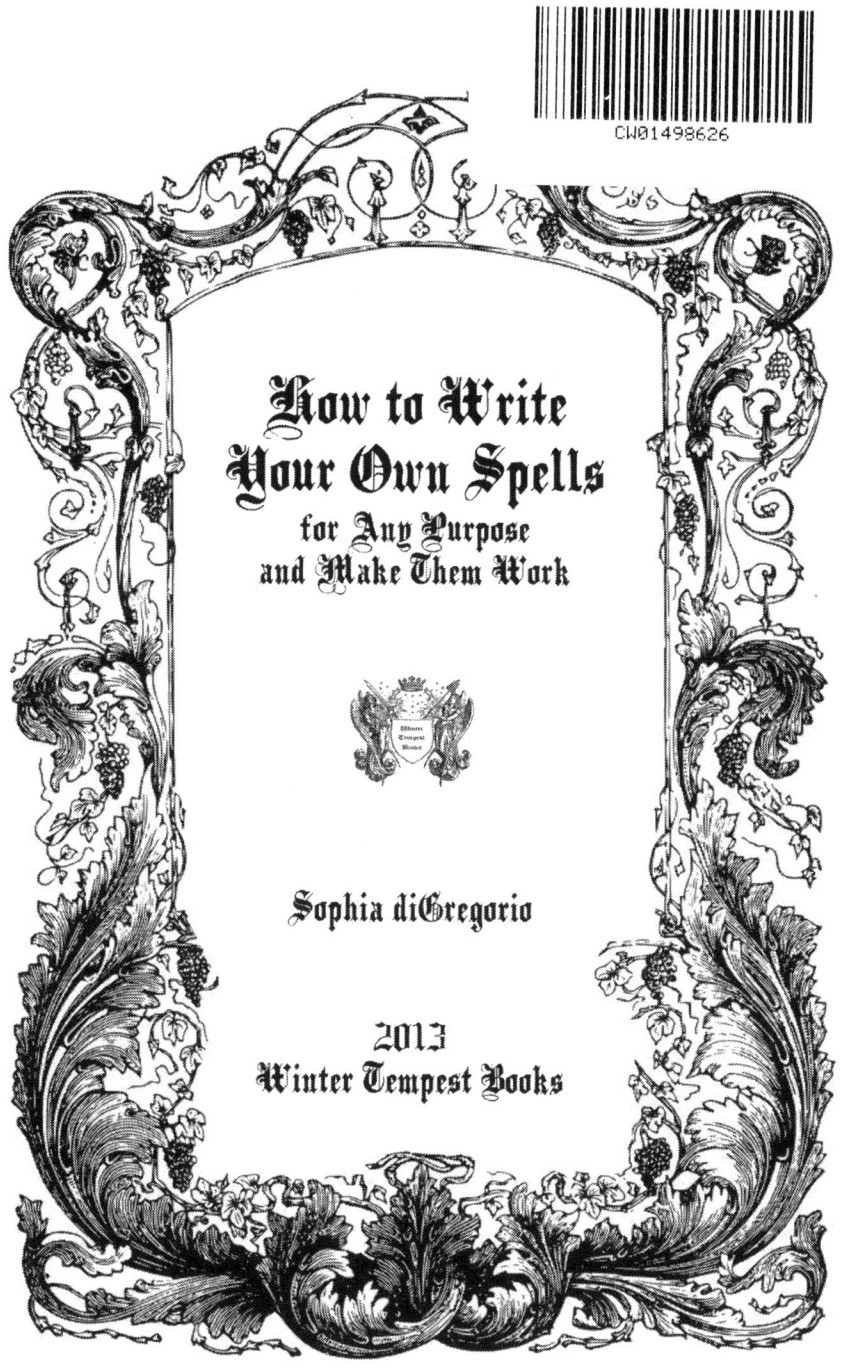

How to Write
Your Own Spells
for Any Purpose
and Make Them Work

Sophia diGregorio

2013
Winter Tempest Books

ISBN: 0615823815
ISBN-13: 978-0615823812
Winter Tempest Books

DEDICATION

In honor of my grandparents.

CONTENTS

PREFACE

The mastery of all aspects of witchcraft is the source of everything; medicine, food, justice, love, money, wealth, success and fulfillment all may be obtained by the knowledge that falls under the heading of "witchcraft." Successful spell casting is an important aspect of witchcraft, an understanding of which leads to a very self-sufficient walk through life. This book approaches spell crafting as the practical application of the esoteric science behind witchcraft. Being able to write and successfully cast your own spells means you will never have problems finding a spell that suits your needs, again.

While spell books are helpful in many cases, the types of spells they provide are usually limited to popular subjects, like love, money and protection, when you may have other needs. They often fail to provide a spell for your particular situation and its unique dynamics. Furthermore, many modern spell books try to impose the author's morality upon the reader and may not contain certain types of spells, at all.

Furthermore, pre-written spells may be either too simple or too complex for your level of mastery. Depending on your skills, problems can sometimes be addressed very directly, while at other times you may need a more complex procedure to achieve your goal.

Both old and new pre-written spells sometimes call for hard-to-find items or call for you to do something dangerous or impossible to complete them. In such cases, you may wish to alter the procedure, but may not be sure how to do it without causing it to fail.

By using the information in this book, whenever you are unable to locate a suitable existing spell, you will be able to write one from scratch. Moreover, you will be able to confidently adjust existing spells to better meet your needs.

It is an inherent limitation of pre-written spells that they can only illustrate a procedure or formula intended to produce a certain result in a narrowly defined circumstance. By contrast, this book helps you to master every aspect of spell casting by giving you an overview of the anatomy of spells and the nature of the forces that propel them so you can write spells perfectly tailored to any situation whatsoever.

This book clarifies the process of writing your own spells and teaches you why certain components are employed and what their purpose is. It shows that there is far more to spell casting than just going through the motions or wishing for a result. All spells have a far greater chance of success when the spell caster has a complete understanding of what he or she is doing and why. Blindly following a procedure or formula without knowledge or going through the motions without understanding is less likely to lead to a positive result.

The spells you write, along with information about the results of their execution, should become part of your own personal, private Book of Shadows. Keeping records of your endeavors and their success or failure is an important method of tracking your progress and improving your skills.

This book is both a manual and a workbook that provides lessons followed by questions and answers. The final chapter shows you how to put the information you have learned in the book together to design your own spells for any purpose.

WHAT IS A SPELL?

A spell is a formula or procedure that is designed to cause a certain effect or exert an influence on a person, circumstance or event. The methods of construction and execution of spells vary, but all are based on the same occult scientific principles involving sympathetic magic and the application of an occult force.

Spells can be cast for virtually any purpose including healing, harming, to attract love, for money, long life, exorcism and protection. They are cast to affect other people and situations and sometimes ourselves, for example, to break habits or rewire our subconscious thinking. They typically employ astrological timing, the energetic harmonic of color, incantation, particular movements, effigies, candles, herbs, potions and sometimes invocation or evocation.

Some, but not all, spells call for the assistance of spirits to aide the operation. In witchcraft, this is sometimes called a conjuration and it is similar to a prayer. Prayer, also, bears a close resemblance to incantation, which is part of spell casting. Incantation is used to appeal to energetic intelligences, which might be regarded as elementals or natural spirits and to direct the energy involved in an operation.

In some traditions, particularly American Hoodoo and Mexican

Witchcraft, standard Catholic prayers are often used, even in black magic rituals. Set prayers such as the Our Father, Hail Mary and the Glory Be are used in spells and are said before addressing saints, including folk saints like Santa Muerte (Holy Death).

Some people confuse spells with affirmations. Affirmations are positive statements intended to affect a person's own subconscious mind. By contrast, spells are not just positive thoughts, but are procedures generally intended to affect the outer environment or other people. While they can cause positive changes in the subconscious mind of the spell caster, this is not usually the purpose.

Spell casting is about more than just promoting the spiritual growth of the spell caster. It is primarily concerned with altering external circumstances in the spell caster's life. More often than not, these are of a physical rather than spiritual nature. Although, successfully mastering the art of spell casting is personally beneficial in that it can lead to greater understanding of the nature of the world both physically and metaphysically.

Spell Procedure

Every spell should have an objective, an object to be acted upon, actions to be taken, power and release. These five following components of a spell are best described as follows:

1. A clearly defined objective. This is your detailed purpose, which may include an entire strategy for accomplishing your goal.

2. The object, situation or entity to be acted upon or its representative, which is called a "Passive Substitution." Examples of this include an effigy, a charm or the person or thing, itself.

3. The action you want to take on the object. This is accomplished by means of an "Active Substitution," which represents the influence you want to bring to bear to the situation, often through the use of candles, colors, potions, incantation. It may, also, be accomplished by means of an "Imitative Action," which is an act that mimics your intention.

4. The empowerment of the spell, which comes from an energy source within the spell caster and sometimes through the assistance of spirits

5. A final, complete release of energy, often including a disposal of the remains of the working, which is appropriate to the spell's purpose.

Always begin by establishing your objective. Know exactly what it is you want to achieve. Then, determine the best way of achieving it based on the information you have, the people involved, your degree of access to them and other variables.

Most spells apply the esoteric principles of sympathetic magic and the force of the will, which are elegantly expressed by Aleister Crowley in the famous quote, "Love is the law, love under will." Love means resonance, harmony or an energy with a quality similar to that you want to work with. Love under will is a reference to directing this energy by means of your mental emanations.

Specific herbs, minerals and other objects are employed in spells because of their innate energy. If you apply this similar energy to an object that has the same or similar energy to the object you are trying to affect, for example, yourself, your business or your home, then you are affecting one energetic form by another through sympathetic magic. Distance healing, also, works on the same principles, so does distance harming.

Every spell should be conducted with the most energy you can conjure and direct into the operation. After you have put a great deal of energy into your spell, you must release it. Essentially, this is done by emitting either a burst or a sustained flow of energy, then afterward forgetting about the entire issue. This is why you are frequently instructed to bury an object or place it somewhere to be forgotten.

This final step is important. Once a spell has been performed, if the energy involved is held onto by the spell caster, it will never have the opportunity to work. Your will must be released into the outer environment to influence the universal vibrational field. In many spells it is released through burning and allowing the essence of the charge to be carried through the air, liquid being poured out into the earth, or the refuse of the spell is buried or hidden.

Your Work Space or Altar

While spells may be performed in many different locales and situations, the primary work space is your personal altar, which should become a center of power.

There is no one right or wrong way to arrange an altar, but the items chosen are usually cleansed and consecrated to your purpose. Afterward, these items are used only in the performance of spells and rituals.

The following are items commonly placed on altars:

Athame (double-edged knife used for ceremonial purposes)
Candles and candle holders
Cauldron
Censer or Thurible (incense burner)
Chalice
Crucible
Images and other symbolic representations of helpful spirits
Wands for different purposes such as ceremonial or for the direction of specific types of energy

Typically, the elements are represented in some way.

Earth: Salt and sometimes a pentacle, which is, also, used to represent the fifth element

Air: The wand and incense

Fire: The athame and flame of the candle

Water: A cauldron or goblet filled with water

These representative objects are sometimes employed to charge other objects. For example, an object may be charged with each of the elements by sprinkling it with salt, passing it through incense, passing it through the flame of a candle and sprinkling it with water.

After you have spiritually cleansed a ritual item by some method, such as White sage (Salvia apiana) smudging, in which you pass the item through the smoke of this herb, consecrate it to serve your purpose. For example, as you sprinkle your athame with salt or drops of water or pass its blade through the smoke of incense, say, "I conjure you, O creature of fire and steel, to cause all things as named by me."

By creating an altar and consecrating it, you are setting up the expectation that once at the altar, only certain things such as meditation, rituals, invocations and spell casting are going to take place. This is a good way to both psychologically and energetically reinforce your purpose and strengthen your spell work.

Questions

1. True or False? The primary purpose of a spell is to affect the subconscious mind of the spell caster?

2. Describe the five basic components of a spell.

3. What object can become a source of great power for spell casting?

4. Give your own definition of the word "consecrate."

5. How might you represent the element of air?

Answers

1. False. The primary purpose of a spell is to affect people and things in the outside environment.

2. Every spell should have (1) an objective, (2) an object to be acted upon, (3) action to be taken, (4) power and (5) release.

3. An altar

4. Consecrate: To set aside an item for a particular purpose. The act of consecration generally involves saying a prayer, essentially speaking to the energy of the item to enhance its power and bring it under your will.

5. By a wand or incense smoke

DETERMINING YOUR OBJECTIVE AND PREPARING TO CAST A SPELL

In spell crafting, it is your own wants and needs or those of your client, if you are working on behalf of someone else, that determine your objective.

Be very specific about what you want to accomplish. Write down your purpose and all of the steps involved in achieving it in the most precise and unequivocal terms.

Consider the following:

1. Who or what will be acted upon
2. The nature of the action to be taken
3. The best strategy for accomplishing your purpose

An effective way to define your objective is in the form of a petition. When you write out a request or intention and address it to a spirit, usually a saint, this is called a "petition," however, it is a very good way to state your intention, whether your working involves the assistance of spirits or not.

Sometimes successful spell casting involves both the application of esoteric science and psychology. So, consider the nature of the particular situation and the people involved. Consider their psychological make-up and their motivations in the matter. What are their strengths and weaknesses? If others are involved in the situation, how do they relate to other people?

If you are unsure about some aspect of a situation that is critical to the success of a spell, use divination to acquire important information about it. For example, use a pendulum or tarot cards to obtain details about a particular circumstance and the people involved, which are otherwise unknown to you.

If the target of your spell work is, also, a witch, then you will have to consider any protections this person might have in place and how to counter or circumvent them.

Devising Tiered Strategies

Sometimes it is best to perform two or more spells in a logical progression to achieve the desired result. When you use a tiered strategy to achieve your final objective, the first spell lays the foundation for the second one, the second lays the foundation for the third one and so on in succession, until you reach your final goal.

For example, if you wanted to increase sales for a product, you might first perform a spell to make the product more desirable, followed by a spell to spread the word about the product and finally a spell to compel people to purchase it.

If you wanted to destroy an enemy, you might begin by conducting a spell to weaken the person's physical health; then, conduct a spell to cause confusion so they have no hope of resistance, before performing a final spell intended to strike a grave blow to the person's health, finances or some other aspect of his well-being.

Suppose you have noisy neighbors and you want to make them move. You might begin by conducting a spell to silence them, then another one to cause them to lose their income before performing the final spell to make them move away.

If you wanted to marry someone who was already married to someone else, you might perform a logical progression of spells to better ensure a successful final outcome. For example, begin by performing a foundational spell to cause discord between the two; then another to send the other party out of the house; then another to cause the man or woman you desire to love you; then, finally, perform a spell to obtain a marriage proposal.

Protective Magic

As part of your tiered strategy, it is wise to include some degree of protective magic. This is especially necessary for more advanced magicians, those who heal, work with spirits, perform exorcisms or practice black magic.

Metaphysical security is a lot like security in the physical world. When you do not feel your personal safety is at much risk, you only take basic steps with regard to security. For example, if you live in an apparently safe neighborhood, you might have locks on your doors, but little else to protect you from intrusion. But, if your neighbor's house is broken into and you begin to feel more immediately threatened, then you might take stronger precautions, such as installing stronger locks, alarms or a surveillance system.

In exactly the same way, the amount of protective magic you should employ is relative to the amount you need. If you only engage in occasional practical magic, you may not need much beyond simple home or personal protection by means of a cleansing, anointing or the use of charms.

But, it is not uncommon for a practitioner to be caught off guard at some stage in their development. If things start going wrong, you will have to step up your use of protective magic. For example, if you begin to suffer from the worst symptoms of malefic witchcraft, such as bad luck or health problems, you will need to use more aggressive methods.

It is always better to err on the side of caution, but it is experience that teaches most witches how much protection they really need at any given time.

Preparing to Cast Spells

It is beneficial to cleanse adverse vibrations from your home or yourself before you cast spells of any kind. Traditionally, people use incense, anointing oil, Holy Water and house washes to cleanse unwholesome vibrations from a place.

The following is an example of a potion used to cleanse a house of adversarial energies:

House Cleansing and Protection

1 gallon water
1/2 cup peppermint
1/4 cup angelica root
1/4 cup basil
1/4 cup sage
1/4 cup hyssop

Combine the above ingredients and bring them to a boil. Reduce the heat and allow this potion to simmer for several minutes. After it is cooled, strain it and use it to wash down the floors and walls inside your home as well as the porch and sidewalk outside. Afterward, dampen a cloth with a few drops of this formula and wipe down all of the smaller surfaces inside your home to cleanse them of their old adversarial vibrations and bring new ones, which are harmonious with your purpose.

Alternatively, you may smudge each corner of a house with a bundle of White sage to cleanse the vibratory field.

In order to cleanse a specific space for a working, some practitioners cast a circle. Casting a circle is optional for most spells, however, it is something many witches like to do, especially when they feel there are forces working against them or they simply need additional reinforcements. For instance, the Obeah practitioners of Africa and the aboriginal magicians of Australia cast protective circles to facilitate spirit communication. Casting a circle may, also, be helpful to you if you are having difficulty focusing or meditating.

There are many ways to cast a circle ranging from the very simple to the complex. Circle-casting rituals typically incorporate the concept of the four elements, which are the spiritual precursors to life on the physical plane, to protect and form a circle that represents the universe itself with you as the creative force within it. But, your circle does not have to be created through an elaborate ceremony to be effective.

If you feel you need the extra protection and power of a circle, simply draw a circle on the floor using chalk, tape, your ritual knife or simply your finger. Some old conjurers made two concentric circles of a similar size and wrote the names of angels or the Tetragrammaton around the circle's edge.

For the circle to be effective, you must see it as a representative of the universe, with yourself in the center of it as its master. Use this circle to become completely focused on your purpose or as a powerful place from which to plan or conduct your spells or communicate with spirits.

Uncrossing

Uncrossing is a concept that comes from American Hoodoo. Similar terms that might apply would be "spiritual cleansing" or "exorcism." Uncrossing revolves around removing energies attached to a person, including negative thoughts or emotions that may be blocking success. Uncrossing Spells are used in cases where you feel there are energies attached to you that are working against you or that you may be mildly jinxed. Crossed people may experience setbacks and difficulties choosing the right path in life.

At some time, most people experience some degree of being crossed because we all have a tendency to accumulate negative energy. For most people, the procedure for uncrossing is a simple one that may involve nothing more than taking a spiritually cleansing bath over the course of one evening. There are various degrees of this kind of contamination and the degree to which you feel you have been affected by it will determine how much work you need to do to eliminate it.

Uncrossing Spell

An Uncrossing Spell is a mild form of exorcism and like some other spells, they may have to be performed more than once to set a permanent energetic pattern. There can be layers to the negative energies, so it may take time and any number of workings before they are completely purged.

You will need the following:

White candle
Uncrossing Oil (formula below)
Uncrossing Bath (formula below)

Anoint the candle with Uncrossing Oil, using a motion away from you.

Uncrossing Oil

1/2 cup almond oil
7 drops bay oil
7 drops hyssop oil
7 drops lavender oil
7 drops rose oil
7 drops verbena oil
7 drops vetivert oil (or a root may be added to the master bottle)

Make this oil by adding the above drops of essential oil to the almond oil. If you do not have the essential oils, but you have the dried herbs, you may make this formula by adding a handful of each of the herbs to a pint or so of oil and allowing it to remain in a warm place for a couple of weeks. Strain the liquid and place it in a dark bottle with a tight lid. Always store your potions in a cool, dark place.

After you have anointed the candle, take an Uncrossing Bath.

Uncrossing Bath

Make a traditional Uncrossing Bath by brewing a strong tea using a handful each of bay leaves and hyssop blossoms. You may, also, add rose and lavender blossoms for calming and increased protection. Sage and lemon are other herbs commonly used in Uncrossing formulas. Add these herbs or essential oils to your Uncrossing Oil or bath formula at your discretion.

Allow the herbs to boil in a about a half gallon of pure water for several minutes before removing the mixture from the heat. Allow it to cool and strain it before adding any essential oils. Recite the following incantation over the brew before adding it to your bath water:

Purge me with hyssop, and I shall be clean; wash me, and I shall be whiter than snow.

Alternatively, you may, also add a few drops of Uncrossing Oil to plain liquid Castille soap like Dr. Bronner's to make an Uncrossing Bath.

You may use this simple Uncrossing Bath right before conducting any spell. Some practitioners, also, use a bath like this one after working malefic spells to rid themselves of any negative energy they may have acquired.

After you have completed your bath, light your anointed candle and recite Psalm 51 in its entirety, as follows:

Have mercy upon me, O God, according to thy loving kindness; according unto the multitude of thy tender mercies blot out my transgressions.

Wash me thoroughly from mine iniquity, and cleanse me from my sin.

For I acknowledge my transgressions; and my sin is ever before me.

Against thee, thee only, have I sinned, and done this evil in thy sight; that thou mightest be justified when thou speakest, and be clear when thou judgest.

Behold, I was shapen in iniquity; and in sin did my mother conceive me.

Behold, thou desirest truth in the inward parts; and in the hidden part thou shalt make me to know wisdom.

Purge me with hyssop, and I shall be clean; wash me, and I shall be whiter than snow.

Make me to hear joy and gladness; that the bones which thou hast broken may rejoice.

Hide thy face from my sins, and blot out all mine iniquities.

Create in me a clean heart, O God; and renew a right spirit within me.

Cast me not away from thy presence; and take not thy holy spirit from me.

Restore unto me the joy of thy salvation; and uphold me with thy free spirit.

Then will I teach transgressors thy ways; and sinners shall be converted unto thee.

Deliver me from blood guiltiness, O God, thou God of my salvation; and my tongue shall sing aloud of thy righteousness.

O Lord, open thou my lips; and my mouth shall shew forth thy praise.

For thou desirest not sacrifice; else would I give it; thou delightest not in burnt offering.

The sacrifices of God are a broken spirit; a broken and a contrite heart, O God, thou wilt not despise.

Do good in thy good pleasure unto Zion; build thou the walls of Jerusalem.

Then shalt thou be pleased with the sacrifices of righteousness, with burnt offering and whole burnt offering; then shall they offer bullocks upon thine altar.

If you are planning on conducting this ritual for more than one night, snuff out the candle after a couple of hours. Otherwise, simply allow the candle to burn out, secure in the knowledge that, as it does so, it destroys any negative energy that may have surrounded you. Repeat this entire procedure before casting spells or whenever you feel out of sorts, stressed or anxious.

Cleansing your home and uncrossing yourself from time to time will help you succeed at casting other types of spells by reducing interference.

Questions

1. What is a petition?

2. How much protective magic should you use?

3. What is the purpose of a cleansing?

4. What is the purpose of a circle?

5. What is the purpose of an Uncrossing spell?

Answers

1. A written request, usually to a spirit and especially a saint.

2. As much as you need considering the type of work you are doing.

3. To cleanse adverse energies from a place, which might interfere with a working.

4. To provide protection and power

5. It is a mild form of exorcism intended to purge adversarial energies from a person, which could interfere with success in spell casting.

SYMPATHETIC MAGIC

Most spells make use of sympathetic magic. This is the esoteric science of correspondences or similarities between objects. What is at work here is akin to the homeopathic Law of Similars.

The Law of Similars means that we can use things of a comparable energetic vibration to create a desired influence. To do this, we find objects that have a vibrational frequency similar to the type of action we want to bring to bear and we manipulate and exert that force on objects that are vibrationally similar to that which we wish to influence. This is why we make use of plants, minerals or other object that have properties similar to the influences we want to bring to a working.

Whenever it is practical and not illegal, you can act directly on the object or person you intend to influence. An example of this is placing a magical substance in a place where the person you wish to influence must touch it or walk through it.

If you do not have direct access to the object or person, then you must use a sympathetic representation. Effigies, poppets or "voodoo dolls" are commonly used to represent a person to be acted upon in a spell. They are associated with a particular person by means of personal effects, which carry his or her vibration.

For example, if you wanted to influence a person to do a favor for you and you did not have direct access to him, you would obtain something that has his vibrational signature on it. This might be a photograph, blood, hair, nail clippings or a piece of paper he has signed his name on. You might conduct your spell using a doll or candle and include the item with his vibrational signature on it to create a substitute for him.

You would then act upon this object in a way that represents what you want to happen in the physical world. You would influence his personal vibratory rate from a distance using powders, oils and other substances that impart energies that correspond to your purpose.

You might do something to symbolize your domination of him in this matter. You might even use your own blood or other bodily fluids together with a domination potion. If you combine a few drops of your own blood with such a potion, you create a formula that has both your vibrational signature combined with a vibration of domination.

Afterward, you would apply this potion to the substitute object that carries his similar vibration, charge the objects concerned with your energy and impregnate that energy with your will.

In this way, you are distantly influencing his mind and emotions by imposing these sympathetic energies and your will upon an object that carries a similar energetic signature to his own. When you act upon an object that carries a person's energetic vibration, it is as if you are acting upon the actual person.

Passive Substitution

A Passive Substitution is a representation of a person or thing to be acted upon in a spell. In most spells, it is a surrogate or a stand-in for a person you wish to affect and is made to carry his or her vibrational signature by means of sympathetic magic. The vibrational signature is the unique harmonic frequency of a person or thing.

Examples of Common Passive Substitutions:

Dolls
Drawings
Documents
Candles

Examples of Objects and Images Used as Passive Substitutions:

Male figure: A man

Female figure: A woman

Images of sex organs: The sexuality of a person

Image of a married couple: Two people and their relationship

Cords or strings: A person, part of a person or a situation

Cat figures: Luck in any endeavor and sometimes stealth and invisibility

Baphomet: Witchcraft powers

Devil: Power

Skulls: The spirits of death, spirit contact; to cause separation and death; for spells concerning the mind and the head

Snakes: Wisdom and protection

Images of spirits, gods or saints: To make contact with the spirit represented

Personal Effects:

Nail clippings
Hairs of the head and body
Blood
Saliva
Other bodily fluids
Recently worn clothing items, especially underwear

Photographs, especially full body images
Signatures
Writing samples
A piece of paper with the person's name, location and birth date
written on it

An item, such as a ring or pendant, regularly worn or carried by a
person can, also, be a Passive Substitution. The item adapts to the
harmonic frequency of the person with whom it is in long-term contact
and it begins to mimic the person's vibrational signature.

If the object of your spell is an institution or a legal matter, a
document that contains pertinent information may be used. For example,
if you wish to affect a contract, then a copy of the contract can be used as
a Passive Substitution.

Other types of Passive Substitutions represent abstract ideas. For
example, a skull may be used to attain control over and manipulate death,
whether to preserve someone from death or to cause death. Charms or
talismans are, also, a type of Passive Substitution. A charm represents an
intangible objective or an abstract situation, which is to be influenced.
For example, a charm or talisman may be made to represent the abstract
ideas of luck or fate.

The vibrational signature of personal effects can be transferred to an
object by means of contact. For example, when hair, a blood spot or nail
clippings belonging to the person are inserted into it, the doll becomes
the Passive Substitution.

When the Passive Substitution represents a person, attach or insert
any personal effects and christen or baptize the object while naming it in
a small ritual before you proceed. Simply hold the completed object and
say, "I name thee, N." or sprinkle water on it and say, "I baptize the, N.,
in the name of the Father, Son and Holy Ghost."

Color in Sympathetic Magic

Candles, altar dressings, ribbons and sometimes ink may be
incorporated into a spell according to the color corresponding to your
objective. But, color correspondences are not entirely universal and
colors have different associations in different parts of the world.

The following are common correspondences used by neo-pagans in
the U.S., U.K. and other English-speaking countries:

Black: Protection; revenge; exorcism; banishing and the dark arts

Blue: (Jupiter) Occult knowledge; psychic abilities; healing; stability and commitment

Brown: Legal matters; court cases and contracts

Gold: (Sun) Domination; success in career; victory in war; wealth; fame; imparts the energy of the sun

Green: (Venus) Money; prosperity; wealth abundance; good fortune; material success

Orange: (Mercury) Career and legal matters; imparts cleansing energy

Pink: Friendship; kindness; romance and affection; imparts gentle energy

Purple: (Saturn) Higher intuition; spiritualism; psychic abilities; peace; idealism; selflessness

Red: (Mercury) Passion; energy; strength; physical health; courage and sexual potency; imparts vigorous energy

Silver: (Moon) Clairvoyance; intuition; inspiration; astral travel; dreams; divination; money; imparts the energy of the moon

White: Purification; peace and protection; an all-purpose color whenever other colors are not available

Yellow: (Earth) Education; thought; intellectual pursuits; material wealth; memory and inspiration

In the Far East and Latin America, there are slightly different correspondences ascribed to some colors:

Amber: Healing; to break addictions and habits

Black: For revenge; hexing; cursing; exorcism and powerful protection from enemies

Bone: Protection of the home and family

Blue: Luck; gambling and employment

Green: Business; prosperity; legal matters and contracts

Light Blue or Sky Blue: Money and travel

Red: Love; lust; power and vigorous protection

White: To protect children; purification; death, especially of young or unmarried people

Yellow: Money; gambling; to improve business and to protect adults

Colored candles may be regarded as Passive Substitutions when they represent a person, thing or abstract idea to be influenced.

Colors are often applied as Active Substitutions to bring certain influences to bear on an object or situation. For example, in modern witchcraft, colored inks of art are used to write spells based on their purpose: Black ink is used in spells for protection, revenge and the dark arts; green is used in money spells and red is used in spells for love.

In American Hoodoo, washes and other preparations are sometimes dyed based on their purpose, as follows:

Blue: Protection and friends

Red: Luck and protection

Yellow: Money

Active Substitution

An Active Substitution is a representation of the influence you want to create on an object or its Passive Substitution. This may be a potion or other tangible substance.

Examples of Active Substitutions:

Herbs
Minerals
Zoological effects, which are objects related to insects, reptiles, birds and other animals
Personal effects, usually those of the spell caster or the person for whom the spell is cast
Unlimited other substances, which possess a quality similar to the effect you want to produce on the target
Potions containing any of the above substances
Colors according to their correspondences

Some Passive Substitutions are, also, used as Active Substitutions, especially in domination spells. For example, bodily fluids and nail clippings are used to gain control over another person and in spells for protection and to reverse black magic.

Properties of herbs are applied to cause effects based on the metaphysical properties of the particular herb. Old herbals like Culpeper's Complete Herbal, published in 1653, tell the characteristics of various herbs, sometimes by its action alone and other times by its planetary correspondence. Planetary correspondences are simply a means of categorizing the actions of herbs and minerals.

Sometimes the metaphysical properties of plants and minerals are ascertained based on the Doctrine of Signatures, which is the principle that the metaphysical and healing properties of plants and minerals can sometimes be ascertained on the basis of their physical qualities, such as, color, shape of leaves, fruits, blossoms, scent and other characteristics.

"A very old example of [the Doctrine of Signatures] is to be found in the use of mandrake (whose roots resemble the human form) by the Hebrews and Greeks as a cure for sterility; or, to give an instance which is still accredited by some, the use of eye-bright (Euphrasia officinalis, L., a plant with a black pupil-like spot in its corolla) for complaints of the eyes. Allied to this doctrine are such beliefs, once held, as that the lungs of foxes are good for bronchial troubles, or that the heart of a lion will endow one with courage; as Cornelius Agrippa put it, 'It is well known amongst physicians that brain helps the brain, and lungs the lungs.'"[1]

Other types of Active Substitutions include household, agricultural and other mundane items based on their ordinary function. For example, in traditional Western witchcraft, a sieve is used to cause rain because it creates drops of water and scissors are employed in spells to cut someone's power.

Zoological Effects

Zoological effects are objects related to insects, reptiles, birds and other animals and may include feet, paws, tails, hooves, horns, skulls, fur, feathers, wings, penises, skins, their dwellings, their feces and urine. They are used as Active Substitutions by applying them to the object you want to affect.

The use of Zoological Effects in witchcraft is well-characterized by James Frazer in *The Golden Bough*:

"Thus some Bechuanas [members of the Batswana nation of South Africa, related to the Bantu] wear a ferret as a charm, because, being very tenacious of life, it will make them difficult to kill. Others wear a certain insect, mutilated, but living, for a similar purpose. Yet other Bechuana warriors wear the hair of a hornless ox among their own hair, and the skin of a frog on their mantle, because a frog is slippery, and the ox, having no horns, is hard to catch; so the man who is provided with these charms believes that he will be as hard to hold as the ox and the frog. Again, it seems plain that a South African warrior who twists tufts of rat's hair among his own curly black locks will have just as many chances of avoiding the enemy's spear as the nimble rat has of avoiding things thrown at it; hence in these regions rats' hair is in great demand when war is expected."

"When you are playing the one-stringed lute, and your fingers are stiff, the thing to do is to catch some long-legged field spiders and roast them, and then rub your fingers with the ashes; that will make your fingers as lithe and nimble as the spiders' legs—at least so think the Galelareese. To bring back a runaway slave an Arab will trace a magic circle on the ground, stick a nail in the middle of it, and attach a beetle by a thread to the nail, taking care that the sex of the beetle is that of the fugitive. As the beetle crawls round and round, it will coil the thread about the nail, thus shortening its tether and drawing nearer to the centre at every circuit. So by virtue of homoeopathic magic the runaway slave will be drawn back to his master."

The power of a particular animal can be used to ward off that animal or any abstraction of its characteristics. For example, "Among the western tribes of British New Guinea, a man who has killed a snake will burn it and smear his legs with the ashes when he goes into the forest; for no snake will bite him for some days afterwards."[2]

Further information about the properties of specific herbs, minerals, Zoological effects and other materials may be found in the *Appendix*.

Principle of Transference

The Principle of Transference, sometimes called "contagious magic," refers to the transmission of the energy of a substance to an object either by physical contact or symbolic association.

The following are examples of the Principle of Transference:

It is practiced by the Bantus when they dig up the grave of an intelligent man and rub their faces with his brain matter to increase their own intelligence before engaging in important business transactions.

In Catholicism, the relics of saints are touched to medals to transfer their vibrational signature to the objects.

The Principle of Transference is involved in the Mexican limpia, in which the vibrations of disease, spiritual attachments or the Evil Eye are transferred from a sick person to an egg.

Baptizing a good luck charm in the name of an extremely wealthy person creates a transfer of his or her fortunate energy to the object. This is an example of causing a transfer of energy by symbolic association.

Transference of energy sometimes takes place inadvertently, as well, which is why witches, especially healers and exorcists, take steps to protect themselves from it.

Imitative Action

An Imitative Action is a physical act that mimics the effect you want to bring to bear on the object of a spell.

For example, to perform a healing spell, act on the Passive Substitution just as you would act on the body of the person if they were present. For example, perform a psychic healing treatment that affects the chakra centers and the vital organs or perform an acupuncture treatment on the energy meridians.

If you wanted to destroy the health of a person, you would act on the Passive Substitution by burning parts of it, causing it to melt or erode, depending on the substance it was made of. You would leave it somewhere unpleasant to rot or be eaten by natural predators or drive nails into parts of it to cause pain.

If you wanted to confuse your target, you would imitate this action in some way, such as twirling the Passive Substitution on a string. To stifle and frustrate a person, you would create an effigy as a Passive Substitution, then cover its eyes, bind its hands and feet, tape its mouth shut and turn its face to the wall.

To keep someone who is in jail imprisoned, put the Passive Substitution in a cage with a key and turn the key every day. To drown them either literally or figuratively, immerse it in water. To suffocate them, poke it down into a container of sand.

To dominate someone, take an action to symbolize your dominance such as placing your influence over the top of theirs. In American Hoodoo, this is done by writing your name over the top of theirs or by placing an item that has the person's influence attached to it beneath your right (dominant) foot by putting it in your shoe.

Conversely, to free someone, you might capture an insect or a bird, baptize it in the name of the person to be liberated and then set it free.

Historical examples of the use of this kind of Imitative Action are given by Sir James George Frazer in *The Golden Bough*:

"For example, when an Ojebway Indian desires to work evil on any one, he makes a little wooden image of his enemy and runs a needle into its head or heart, or he shoots an arrow into it, believing that wherever the needle pierces or the arrow strikes the image, his foe will the same instant be seized with a sharp pain in the corresponding part of his body; but if he intends to kill the person outright, he burns or buries the puppet, uttering certain magic words as he does so. The Peruvian Indians moulded images of fat mixed with grain to imitate the persons whom they disliked or feared, and then burned the effigy on the road where the intended victim was to pass. This they called burning his soul."

"A Malay charm of the same sort is as follows. Take parings of nails, hair, eyebrows, spittle, and so forth of your intended victim, enough to represent every part of his person, and then make them up into his likeness with wax from a deserted bees' comb. Scorch the figure slowly by holding it over a lamp every night for seven nights, and say: 'It is not wax that I am scorching, It is the liver, heart, and spleen of So-and-so that I scorch.' After the seventh time burn the figure, and your victim will die."[3]

An example of the use of zoological effects combined with Imitative Action is the use of a cow's tongue in spells to "shut up" an enemy. Beef tongue is baptized to become the tongue of the enemy and it is then acted upon by means of needles or nails to sew it up or immobilize it, after which it is sometimes frozen.

Knots as a Form of Imitative Magic

The binding and loosing of knots in strings, ribbons and cords is an old and powerful form of imitative magic and another example of the use of Imitative Action.

At one time the Finlanders and Laplanders drove a profitable trade by the sale of winds by means of a magical cord. After being paid they knitted three magical knots and told the buyer that when he untied the first, he would have a good gale; when the second, a strong wind; and when the third, a severe tempest.[4]

The "witch's ladder" is another name for the knotted cord in which the cord or string is used as a Passive Substitution to represent a person or an abstract idea. If the cord represents a person, it might be made of his or her own hair fibers. The cord may be cut a certain length that corresponds with a person's body part that you want to control and bodily fluids of the person it represents may be applied to it.

Sympathetic magic is applied to knots using the appropriate Active Substitutions. For example, hair of the person to be affected, feathers, bones, and other items are knotted into place to bind whatever it represents.

Then, Imitative Actions are applied to the knots in the form of knotting to fix or bind a certain quality and loosening knots to release that quality. Recite an incantation, then spit or blow into a knot and tie it. Employ knots to tie down bad luck or to tie loyal friends to you and maintain their loyalty.

Usually the number of knots tied in a single cord is nine or some other odd number, which is beneficial to successful spell casting. Even numbers of knots are generally avoided.

Questions

1. Give an example of a Passive Substitution.

2. Give an example of an Active Substitution.

3. Give an example of a Personal Effect.

4. Name a color used in spells for love and romance.

5. Name a color used in spells for protection.

6. Name a color used in spells for purification.

7. Name the color most commonly used in revenge spells.

8. Name two colors commonly used in spells for money, abundance and wealth.

9. Name a color commonly used in court cases.

10. Name two colors commonly used in spells for psychic enhancement, divination and increased intuition.

11. Name the color that is considered neutral and is used as a substitution when other colors cannot be obtained.

12. Give an example of an Imitative Action.

13. Give an example of a Zoological Effect.

14. Describe the Principle of Transference

Answers

1. A Passive Substitution is acted on in place of a person, thing or an abstract concept. Common examples include Personal Effects, poppets, drawings, a signature, a photograph or anything you use to represent the object of your spell. Also, candles and objects that represent an abstract idea may be used as Passive Substitutions.

2. An Active Substitution may be a potion or other substance, which imparts a similar energy to that of the effect you wish to produce on the object of your spell.

3. A Personal Effect is anything that contains the vibratory signature of your subject and may include hair, blood, saliva, soiled clothing, bodily fluids, a piece of paper with the person's signature on it, a photograph or any object that they have carried with them for a long time.

4. Red or pink

5. White or black and sometimes yellow or red

6. White

7. Black

8. Green, gold or golden yellow

9. Brown or yellow

10. Blue and purple

11. White

12. Imitative Action is an act that mimics the type of action you wish to bring to bear on a subject. Some examples are burning, melting, turning and binding and loosing knots.

13. Zoological Effects are related to animals, insects and reptiles and include such items as fur, feathers, claws and teeth among other things.

14. Transference is the principle of transferring traits or qualities from one person or object to another.

TIMING AND THE DYNAMIC ETHER

According to witchcraft theory, when a spell is performed properly, an energetic signal is sent through the dynamic ether to affect the object of the spell. This signal is similar to a radio wave or a satellite signal that travels through space to a receiver, however, this seemingly empty space is actually a field that it must pass through.

This field, called the dynamic ether, can be influenced by other emanations in the atmosphere causing the signal you have sent to become weakened. These emanations come from atmospheric conditions involving such things as the phase of the moon and the position of the planets.

If you choose the wrong time to conduct your spell, your effort will be a little like trying to sail into a headwind. You might make it to your destination, but the result will be hindered, slower and more difficult. In the worst case, it might be entirely impeded.

Conversely, choosing timing that is harmonious with your purpose can aide your effort because the atmospheric forces are working with you. If your spell is well-timed, the ease of obtaining a positive result can be likened to sailing with the wind at your back, propelling you along.

Important aspects of timing include the day of the week, the planetary hour, other planetary influences, moon phases and the sabbats.

Timing According to Planetary Correspondences

The planetary hours are an ancient, Western system of organizing human affairs using the traditional seven planets. Each planet has a corresponding day and natural energies that are beneficial to the performance of certain types of spells.

For the best results, a spell should be performed during its most energetically harmonious planetary hour.

For example, love spells should be performed in the hour of Venus; Court Case spells in the hour of the Sun or Mars; wealth spells in the hour of Jupiter; spells for binding and cursing in the hour of Saturn, etc.

Choose the best planetary hour at which to conduct your spell based on its purpose, as follows:

Sun (Sunday): Spells for success; fame; illumination; learning; vitality; family; dealing with authority figures and court cases.

Moon (Monday): Spells for the mind; mental health; the home; protection; meditation; prophetic dreams, planting and harvesting and affecting time.

Mars (Tuesday): Spells for increased passion; vigor; aggression; aggressive protection; courage; adventure; the triumph of the will; success in military actions; law suits; conflicts; sports; games and conquering.

Mercury (Wednesday): Spells for communications; higher learning; occult studies; business; acting; the arts; sales and marketing; writing; short trips; deception and con artistry.

Jupiter (Thursday): Spells for prosperity; abundance; growth; expansion; increase; optimism; increased earning; good luck; healing; psychic development and expansion of awareness; investments; settling disputes and giving blessings.

Venus (Friday): Spells for love; friendship; affection; other affairs of the heart; charity; social situations; parties; gatherings; weddings; engagements; romance; beauty and communications with women.

Saturn (Saturday): Spells for binding; shrinking; restricting; decreasing; marriages; contracts; legal matters; to break a habit; chronic illnesses; older people; the dark arts; cursing; hexing, hex breaking; revenge and spell reversal.

The Planetary Hours

After you have chosen the most beneficial planetary hour for your spell, determine its time of day.

The fastest way to calculate planetary hours is with a Planetary Hours Calculator. These little software programs are available at web sites online and as Smartphone applications. You can find the planetary hours for the day or night in an instant. But, you can do it manually, as well.

The day is divided by the daylight hours and the nighttime hours. Each planetary day begins at sunrise and ends at sunset. Each planetary night begins at sunset and ends at sunrise the following day.

Each part of the planetary day is divided into twelve equal "hours."

The same is done for the night. You will have 24 unequal hours between day and night. Rarely will any of your hours actually consist of 60 minutes.

As you can see from The Table of Planetary Hours, which is given below, the first planetary hour of each day corresponds to the day, itself. For example, the first planetary hour of Sunday is always the hour of the Sun; the first planetary hour of Monday is always the hour of the Moon, and so on.

The hours infinitely repeat in the following order: Sun; Venus; Mercury; Moon; Saturn; Jupiter; Mars.

Determine the time of sunrise and sunset for your particular geographic location.

Calculate the number of minutes between sunrise and sunset and divide the sum by 12.

Determine each planetary hour according to the 12 planets listed under that day in the chart below.

To calculate the planetary hours for night time, do the same procedure only instead calculate using the number of minutes from sunset to sunrise.

Table of Planetary Hours

Hour	Sun.	Mon.	Tues.	Wed.	Thurs.	Fri.	Sat.
1	Sun	Moon	Mars	Mercury	Jupiter	Venus	Saturn
2	Venus	Saturn	Sun	Moon	Mars	Mercury	Jupiter
3	Mercury	Jupiter	Venus	Saturn	Sun	Moon	Mars
4	Moon	Mars	Mercury	Jupiter	Venus	Saturn	Sun
5	Saturn	Sun	Moon	Mars	Mercury	Jupiter	Venus
6	Jupiter	Venus	Saturn	Sun	Moon	Mars	Mercury
7	Mars	Mercury	Jupiter	Venus	Saturn	Sun	Moon
8	Sun	Moon	Mars	Mercury	Jupiter	Venus	Saturn
9	Venus	Saturn	Sun	Moon	Mars	Mercury	Jupiter
10	Mercury	Jupiter	Venus	Saturn	Sun	Moon	Mars
11	Moon	Mars	Mercury	Jupiter	Venus	Saturn	Sun
12	Saturn	Sun	Moon	Mars	Mercury	Jupiter	Venus

Timing by Phases of the Moon

The moon has a powerful effect on the earth's energies. Many practitioners believe the moon phase is one of the most important considerations in the timing of magical endeavors.

The phases of the moon can be determined through personal observation, by consulting almanacs or using Moon Phase software or applications for your computer or Smartphone.

Determine the best moon phase during which to conduct your spell based on its purpose.

New Moon: This phase runs from the first day of the New Moon to 3 1/2 days after. It is a good time to conduct spells for new beginnings and new ventures including new love affairs, new businesses and the formation of new habits.

Waxing Moon: This phase begins 7 days after the New Moon and lasts for 7 days after. It is the right time to conduct spells for positive purposes such as increased money and prosperity, to gain something you want, to acquire love, to foster friendships, to improve health, wealth, luck, love and success.

Full Moon: This phase begins 14 days after the New Moon and lasts 3/12 days. It is a good time to conduct spells for divination, protection, love, legal matters, financial betterment, increased energy and empowerment.

Waning Moon: This phase begins 3 1/2 days after the Full Moon and lasts for 10 1/2 days. It is the right time to conduct spells involving the dark arts, to bind, get revenge, break a habit and to banish a problem, a pest, enemy or an unwanted lover.

The Moon in the Zodiac Signs

Another way to determine the best time to conduct a spell is based on the characteristics of the moon in the astrological signs. Witches' almanacs provide the signs of the moon throughout the calendar year and some web sites offer "Moon Sign Calculators" with which you can quickly calculate the position of the moon for any day of the year.

Determine the best time to conduct your spell according to the position of the moon in the astrological signs, as follows:

Moon in Aries: Spells for money; to get a job; increase sales; improve business; for vigorous strength; domination; courage and passion. Avoid conducting spells for divination at this time.

Moon in Taurus: Spells for matters pertaining to love; friendship; financial matters; determination; strength; real estate and practical, every day matters.

Moon in Gemini: Spells related to travel; learning; communication; sales; acting; public relations and healing.

Moon in Cancer: Spells related to the home; loyalty; intuition; sympathy; fertility; family and children.

Moon in Leo: Spells for fame; careers; success; to gain power over others; for courage and childbirth. Avoid conducting spells for love or relationships at this time.

Moon in Virgo: Spells revolving around learning; healing; employment; health; the intellect; security and stability.
Moon in Libra: Spells pertaining to legal matters; marriages; court cases; partnerships and peace keeping.

Moon in Scorpio: Spells for divination; necromancy; psychic experiences; psychic development; spirit communication; the dark arts; secrets; power and sexual matters.

Moon in Sagittarius: Spells involving travel; publishing; athletic events and learning. Avoid conducting spells for divination or psychic enhancement at this time.

Moon in Capricorn: Spells for domination; career; politics; ambition; material wealth; control and stability.

Moon in Aquarius: Spells for healing; peace; harmony; freedom; science; emotional attachments; to find creative solutions and for understanding.

Sabbats

The eight Sabbats are times when powerful cosmic rays strike the earth. You may choose times on or near these dates to conduct spells for added potency.

Beltane or May Day: April 30th
Litha, Midsummer's Eve or Summer Equinox: June 21st
Lughnassadh: August 1st
Mabon or Autumn Equinox: September 21st
Halloween or Samhain: October 31st
Yule or Winter Equinox: December 21st
Imbolc or Candlemas: February 2nd
Ostara or Spring Equinox: March 21st

Significance of Numbers in Witchcraft

Odd numbers are intimately associated with witchcraft and especially the dark arts. In particular, the influence of the number three and its multiples is beneficial to the success of a spell.

Spells for any purpose may be successfully performed at three o'clock, nine o'clock or midnight. Nine is especially powerful, being the result of three times three and twelve is powerful because it is the numerological equivalent of three because $1 + 2 = 3$.

Of all the numbers arithmeticall,
The number three is heald for principall,
As well in naturall philosophy,
As supernaturall theologie.

The energy of the number three is incorporated into a spell in different ways, such as the repetition of incantations three times, ingredients in potions numbering three, offerings to spirits in threes or stirring a potion three times.

"The Bavarian peasant, in passing through a haunted place, considers himself amply fortified against evil if he takes the precaution to carry three things; namely, (1) a new knife which has never cut anything, marked on the blade with three crosses; (2) a loaf of bread baked on Epiphany Eve; (3) a black cat."[5]

Seven is considered a fortunate number, capable of attracting good luck and dispelling adversity and evil. The following are historical examples of the incorporation of the number seven into charms and spells:

"A Hindu woman, on returning with her young child from a strange village, is careful, before entering her own dwelling, to pass seven small stones seven times around the baby's head, and throw them away in different directions, in order thus to disperse any evil which may have been contracted during her trip."

"And as a preliminary to other mystic procedures, in order to avert the Evil Eye, the Hindus wave around the patient's face seven pebbles taken from a spot where three roads meet, seven leaves of the date-palm, and seven bunches of leaves of the bor tree."

"The employment of odd numbers in magical formulae is exemplified in the following recipe for a drink against all temptations of the Devil, used by the Saxons in England: Take betony, bishopwort, lupins, githrife, attorlothe, wolfscomb, yarrow; lay them under the altar, sing nine masses over them, scrape the worts into holy water, give the man to drink at night, fasting, a cup-full, and put the holy water into all the meat which the man taketh. Work thus a good salve against the temptations of the fiend."

Nine equals the sum of three times three and is thus very powerful in all spells and charms. The following is an example of the use of the number nine in an old anti-witchcraft charm from Scotland:

"Then they tied nine rusty nails to a cord with nine knots on it. This cord they tied to the chain on the cow's neck, and then went away."[6]

The creation of the classic formula Love Potion No. 9 is an example of a spell in which the number nine is incorporated into every act associated with its performance. The potion contains nine herbs. It is stirred nine times. The incantation, which invokes nine spirits, is repeated nine times. It is performed at the ninth hour of the ninth day of the ninth month.

Eleven is a gateway between the world of the physical and the metaphysical. It is associated with spirit manifestation and spirit communication.

With regard to the power of odd numbers in witchcraft, the much maligned number thirteen is the exception to the rule. Thirteen is a powerful number associated with both good and bad luck and particularly with the reversal of fortune; it is, also, associated with death and change. Numerologically, it reduces to the number four, which is a number of densely physical energy.

The number thirteen did not fall into disrepute in Western Europe until the calculation of the calendar changed. "When the year was reckoned as thirteen lunar months of twenty-eight days each, the number thirteen, according to one view, was considered auspicious; but when, under the present method of solar time, the number of months was reduced to twelve, thirteen's reputation was changed for the worse." [7]

Consider these numbers and their associations when determining the appropriate timing and other components of spells.

Questions

1. Name a good day of the week or planetary hour for casting a spell for increasing occult knowledge.

2. Name a good day of the week or planetary hour for casting a spell for success in any endeavor.

3. Name a good day of the week or planetary hour for casting a spell to improve psychic abilities.

4. Name a good day of the week or planetary hour for casting a spell to break a bad habit, break a curse or break a contract.

5. What is the first planetary hour of Sunday?

6. Calculate the planetary hour of Saturn during the daylight if today is Monday and sunrise occurs at 6:50 a.m. and sunset occurs at 4:32 p.m.

   A. The number of minutes between 6:50 a.m. and 4:32 p.m. is _____?

   B. This number divided by 12 is _____?

   C. How long is each hour of daylight on this day?

   D. When does the first hour of Saturn begin?

   E. When does the second hour of Saturn begin?

7. What is a good moon phase for banishing an unwanted person?

8. What is a good moon phase for improving your finances?

9. What is a good moon phase for starting a new business or other endeavor?

10. The moon in which astrological house is an ideal time for casting a spell for family or fertility?

11. The moon in which astrological house is an ideal time for casting a spell for domination?

12. Even numbered hours of the day are generally considered fortunate times for casting spells. True or false?

13. The number _____ and its multiples are considered by many practitioners to be the most fortunate for casting successful spells.

Answers

1. Wednesday

2. Sunday or Tuesday

3. Monday

4. Saturday

5. The Hour of the Sun.

6.

 A. The number of minutes between 6:50 a.m. and 4:32 p.m. is 9 hours and 42 minutes or 582 minutes.

 B. Divided by 12 equals 48 1/2.

 C. Each hour of daylight on this day is 48 1/2 minutes long.

 D. On a Monday, the hour of Saturn occurs during the second and ninth hours. So, the first hour of Saturn occurs 48/12 minutes after 6:50 a.m., which is at 7:38 1/2 a.m. and lasts until 8:27 a.m.

 E. The second hour of Saturn on this same day (Monday) occurs at 1:18 p.m. and lasts until 2:06 1/2 p.m.

The following is a list of the 12 daytime planetary hours for a Monday on which sunrise occurs at 6:50 a.m. and sunset occurs at 4:32 p.m. and each planetary hour is 48 1/2 minutes long:

 1st hour is the Hour of the Moon and begins at 6: 50 a.m. and ends at 7:38 1/2 a.m.
 2nd hour is the Hour of Saturn and begins at 7:38 1/2 a.m. and ends at 8:27 a.m.
 3rd hour is the Hour of Jupiter and begins at 8:27 a.m. and ends at 9:15 1/2 a.m.
 4th hour is the Hour of Mars and begins at 9:15 1/2 a.m. and ends at 10:04 a.m.
 5th hour is the Hour of the Sun and begins at 10:04 a.m. and ends at 10:52 1/2 a.m.

6th hour is the Hour of Venus and begins at 10:52 1/2 a.m. and ends at 11:41 a.m.

7th hour is the Hour of Mercury and begins at 11:41 a.m. and ends at 12:29 1/2 p.m.

8th hour is the Hour of the Moon and begins at 12:29 1/2 p.m. and ends at 1:18 p.m.

9th hour is the Hour of Saturn and begins at 1:18 p.m. and ends at 2:06 1/2 p.m.

10th hour is the Hour of Jupiter and begins at 2:06 p.m. 1/2 and ends at 2:55 p.m.

11th hour is the Hour of Mars and begins at 2:55 p.m. and ends at 3:43 1/2 p.m.

12th hour is the Hour of the Sun and begins at 3:43 1/2 p.m. and ends at 4:32 p.m.

7. New Moon or Waning Moon

8. Full or Waxing Moon

9. New Moon

10. Moon in Cancer

11. Moon in Capricorn

12. False

13. 3

THE POWER OF WITCHCRAFT

Without the power to make it work, a spell is only a series of empty actions. A witch's power is complex. It comes from sources within and without. Some people are born with a great deal of natural power, while others are born with less. All witches can develop and increase their power by studying, practicing and being open to power sources outside themselves.

A witch's power comes from three main sources: Knowledge; skill and spiritual aide.

KNOWLEDGE

The knowledge base for witchcraft is very large and there is no prescribed method of going about learning what is really a lifetime pursuit.

Many popular books on the subject of modern witchcraft lead people to the study of the Wiccan religion and do not proceed beyond the boundaries of Wicca, which has become very popular and is glamorized in movies. While it is important to look at all aspects of witchcraft, including Wicca, to get an overview of witchcraft, any serious study of the subject must go deeper than that which is popular and superficial. In many cases, popular culture's glamorized portrayal of witchcraft in movies and television programs has created some obstacles, which include a lot of misinformation and fantasy. Anyone interested in obtaining knowledge and the power that is derived from it must be prepared to look beyond the glamorous facade of popular witchcraft and delve into the most obscure regions of the occult.

In your pursuit of occult knowledge, do not be distracted by religion or social issues. Witchcraft is not a political or social statement any more than it is a fashion statement. It is a science based on universal truths and it knows no race, gender or sexual preference.

The purpose of witchcraft studies is to understand the true nature of the universe, including how all things, down to the tiniest atom, came into being. Since no one knows this exactly, we rely on a base of occult knowledge left to us by ancient people and on a set of theories or hypotheses, similar to those that exist in orthodox science, but which are slightly different. They are, however, working theories, which is why they are given credence.

The unsettling fact inherent to the pursuit of the knowledge of witchcraft is that you may never arrive at a definitive answer to all of your questions. Unlike religion, in which theories are taken on faith without evidence, it provides no dogmas which are held to be the end all and be all answers to the questions of the universe. In the pursuit of occult knowledge, we only suppose, experiment based on those suppositions and look to see if we achieve results or not. We base our conclusions on the outcome and when we find out we were wrong about something we previously supposed, we acknowledge the error and cast the idea aside in search of the right answer.

These suppositions and theories are not based on wild imagination, but on ancient systems which attempt to explain how things came to be. Witches study the physical and metaphysical nature of the world and attempt to redirect the forces involved in the process of creation to effect their own will.

Spell casting is never about mind over matter; it is always about mind (or mental emanations) over energy. When a spell is cast and the action takes place upon a person, the action does not take place on the physical matter of the person or on his or her physical body. It takes place on the subtle energetic field, which is causal to the physical body. This is the etheric body, although, in occult literature it is known by other names. The body and all living things are comprised of two basic types of energy. There is the electrostatic energy of the physical tissues. Then, there is the vital energy, which passes through those tissues.

When a spell is cast to affect a non-living entity, an institution or an abstract idea, a similar process takes place. It is always the energetic field of a thing, a thought, an emotion or an idea that is affected, which is causal to the thing itself, but not the actual, physical thing. The whirling particles of energy, in the sea of wave emanations in which we all exist, both produces energy and can be acted upon by the production of a willfully directed force of energy.

Now, just as it was historically, witchcraft presents challenges not only to religious establishments, but to the established institutions of science and medicine. This fact was the cause of much of the persecution in the past, and despite a popular notion to the contrary, it still persists today because alternative science and alternative health are two related areas of study that have a lot in common with witchcraft.

The Occult Scientific Basis of Western Witchcraft

Great advances in science were made in the 19th and 20th centuries. But, it was in the latter part of the 19th century that the official science diverged into a philosophy of materialism and related theories and the study of medicine went along with it. There had already been a great divide in medicine between allopathy (conventional medicine) and homeopathy stemming from the days of George Washington, however, as the governmental power structure in the U.S. grew stronger, science and the limits and boundaries to which it could be explored were curtailed by the establishment.

Modern-day official science is very much like a religious cult with its priests and its zealots who shout down any idea that falls outside their accepted view of physics, biology or medicine. They hold on to their narrow-minded and unproven theories despite the fact that modern technology belies their materialist view of the world.

Nikola Tesla the Wizard of the West

One of the greatest scientists of all time was Nikola Tesla who is responsible for many of the modern devices and technology we take for granted today. Among his most common household inventions are the radio and the battery. His system of alternating current electricity made the modern use of electricity, as we know it today, possible. Tesla posited a scientific view of the world that is very much like the esoteric science of witchcraft. He saw the world as being fundamentally comprised of waves of energy, which could be described mathematically in terms of frequency.

Because of his unorthodox views, he was maligned and died in poverty and obscurity, with other men like Thomas Edison and Guglielmo Marconi receiving credit for his inventions. Meanwhile, the scientific orthodoxy skeptically shook its collective head because it could not understand his theories, which are truly elementary to anyone familiar with the occult.

Without the wave and frequency theories of Tesla, computers, satellites, radio, television and virtually any technology that involves the passing of a signal through the dynamic ether would not exist. Yet, the theories of Nikola Tesla are ridiculed by the priesthood of the scientific orthodoxy, which has attempted to suppress not only Tesla's witchcraft-like scientific theories, but a host of related scientific innovations that threaten their power structure and their world view.

A common emotional reaction to Tesla's theories is that, if they are true, then they present a danger to frightening to be contemplated. This is nothing new - the science of witchcraft has always terrified the ignorant. If, for example, it is true (and it is) that by means of a frequency harmonic an individual person can be singled out and acted upon at a distance by means of an electromagnetic wave of energy, then this is a frightening prospect, which some people prefer to simply put out of their minds. Although, Tesla's theories of waves and electromagnetic frequencies have extremely broad applications, the black magic of national defense is one of the areas where they have been covertly applied by the establishment, which may be another reason this branch of science has been suppressed.

Nikola Tesla is sometimes referred to as the "Wizard of the West." This characterization is in no way hyperbolic. Anyone who undertakes a study of his life and work is likely to be surprised at the contrast between the truth of the history of modern science and the academic text book version of these events. The Tesla Memorial Society of New York (www.teslasociety.com) provides a good resource for information about this enigmatic man. Tesla, also, applied for a large number of patents, which are all in the public domain.

Witchcraft Medicine

The orthodox scientific view of the world is that it is constructed of various states and degrees of matter. By contrast, in esoteric science, we see that the world is comprised of various degrees, densities, frequencies and harmonics of energy.

When the same principles of esoteric science used in spell crafting are applied to the healing arts, we have very often the best chance to observe and gauge results and really see how these scientific theories work when they are properly applied. Through the practice of healing, especially through the use of technology based on the occult science of waves and frequencies, that the esoteric science of witchcraft ceases to be theoretical. It is by making practical use of these principles that you come to know them, not as a matter of faith, but a matter of fact.

One of the earliest recorded Western modes of healing is through the use of herbs, minerals and other natural substances. Systems were devised for understanding and categorizing the powers of specific herbs and minerals on the basis of astrology and numerology. The 15th century occultist Henry Cornelius Agrippa's work on this subject, *Three Books of Occult Philosophy*, became the foundation for his successors.

Various means are used to extract the active properties from plants and minerals. Beyond tinctures, teas, steam distillation, grinding and powdering are methods related to the ancient Hermetic science of alchemy, such as spagyria.

The science of creating spagyric remedies was practiced and documented by Theophrastus Bombastus von Hohenheim, later known as Paracelsus, in the 16th century. It was upon the foundation of this alchemical process that Samuel Hahnemann developed the healing system of homeopathy.

Homeopathy works on the very same principles of esoteric science involving waves and frequency harmonics as spell casting. In fact, sympathetic magic has been called "homeopathic magic" by some old occult writers.

Those who say that witches are no longer persecuted are apparently unaware of the silent war that has been waged on alternative medicine. Alternative health and those who dare to practice it are still being persecuted in the U.S., just as the witches of centuries past, because the scientific and medical establishment, which is enmeshed in the dogma of official medicine based on unproven theories and faulty research methods, lack the education to understand how alternative medicine works. And, because they are the priesthood holders of the religion of official medical doctrine, they refuse to even look at such "heresy," ironically dismissing its practitioners by labeling them quacks.

To the allopath who places his faith in the materialism of the scientific orthodoxy, which theorizes that the world is comprised of matter, a homeopathic remedy is only water with "nothing" in it. But, anyone who understands the principles of esoteric science can see how a frequency harmonic is imprinted upon the atoms of the water, which are themselves composed of energy.

Radionics

Radionics takes the concept of homeopathy to a technological level in which frequencies can be broadcast to a target. Radionics is even more closely paralleled with the art of spell crafting because it sends radio-like waves to a Passive Substitution, which has the same frequency vibration as the person who is being targeted for treatment. With radionics, homeopathic-like frequencies can be broadcast like a radio signal to a target based on his, her or its individual harmonic frequency.

The inventor of radionics was a chiropractor from Greely, Colorado named Ruth Drown whose work was influenced by the science of radio and MacGregor Mathers' book, *Kabbalah Unveiled.* "The Tree of Life represents symbolically the descent of power from the Great Unmanifest through the various densities of spiritual existence to the physical-material world." Drown understood that the entire cosmos can be described mathematically and this knowledge is encoded into the Kabbalistic Tree of Life. Her system of radionics is the practical application of these principles of occult science through electromagnetic instrumentation.[8]

While Ruth Drown was the inventor, there have been many innovators since the creation of the first radionics machine. At the cutting edge of this technology is CopenLabs. Bruce Copen is the author of many books that illuminate the scientific theory and practice of radionics. (www.copenlabs.com)

It is difficult to find much practical information about radionics in the U.S. because it has been driven underground by government organizations like the FDA and the AMA. Although it is very safe, it is illegal to use radionics to diagnose or treat human beings, however, it is permitted for veterinary and agricultural applications.

To understand radionics, David Tansley's book, Rays and Radionics, should be studied together with A.E. Powell's *The Etheric Double* and other works of the second wave Theosophists. Closely related to the broadcast method of radionics is Edgar Cayce's system of healing disease with colored rays by projecting a light upon a patient through a colored glass.

The old power structure of science and medicine has not changed. And, there must be those at the top of the hierarchy, those who are in the innermost circle, who know the truth because we see this technology applied. But, this knowledge, which is true power, is hoarded by them while false scientific doctrines are taught in the schools and universities. Anyone who discovers this truth becomes a heretic, is marginalized, ridiculed and in some cases eliminated.

To understand how the official science of the medical orthodoxy got its choke hold on the official medicine of the U.S., read the book, *Murder by Injection,* by Eustace Mullins. It outlines the rise of the American Medical Association and related "charitable organizations," in particular the American Cancer Society, whose primary goal is apparently to make money, even at the expense of human suffering and death.

Theosophy

The unacknowledged pioneers of quantum physics were two second wave Theosophists, Annie Besant

and C.W. Leadbeater who wrote about it in 1908 in their book, *Occult Chemistry: Investigations by Clairvoyant Magnification into the Structure of the Atoms of the Periodic Table and Some Compounds.* Werner Heisenberger who is credited with the discovery of quantum mechanics did not set forth his theories until 1925.

The understanding of quantum physics, even at the highest level of academia is full of confusion and illogical theories. The key to understanding it lies in the work of the true pioneers, the metaphysicians and Theosophists Annie Besant and C.W. Leadbeater. As long as their contribution is disregarded by the establishment scientists, the true nature of atoms, particles, waves and frequencies will remain obscured by academia and the priesthood of the scientific orthodoxy.[9]

Unwilling to admit the flaws of orthodox thinking, the scientific establishment begrudgingly conceded a compromise with esoteric scientific reality by concocting the String Theory, which incorporates some indisputable ideas from quantum physics, while still failing to entirely grasp the concept. It is impossible to fully understand quantum physics while still maintaining blind faith in Newtonian science and its theories and methodologies.

Madame Blavatsky was the founder of Theosophy. She authored the books, *The Secret Doctrine* and *Isis Unveiled*, which give a complex, but illuminating set of theories on cosmology, which is the foundation for much of the work of Besant and Leadbeater. She, also, founded a magazine for esoteric thought, called *Lucifer*, in 1887.[10]

Closely related to Theosophy is the esoteric philosophy of Hermeticism, which encompasses a variety of once highly secretive orders that preserved ancient esoteric scientific theories encoded in the Kabbalah. Hermeticism includes a large body of work by occult writers over the centuries, including the classical grimoires.

The Theosophists and the Hermeticists, especially the Golden Dawn, whose stated mission was to disclose that which had long been hidden, made a point of publicizing their knowledge so that all people would have the opportunity to be illuminated by it. Much of their writing now lies in the public domain and is easily accessible in the internet age, so take advantage of this opportunity to educate yourself whenever you can.

The work of Franz Bardon, entitled, *Initiation Into Hermetics,* is among the most illuminating and practical of books ever written on the subject. To get the most out of Bardon's work you should be familiar with, at least, the early lessons in Hermeticism provided by the Hermetic Order of the Golden Dawn in Israel Regardie's book, *The Golden Dawn: The Original Account of the Teachings, Rites & Ceremonies of the Hermetic Order*, which should be studied together with his other work, A Garden of Pomegranates. Many beginners like to leap past the intense study phase and into going through the motions of the rituals, but these are useless without the initial study. Impatient beginners who enjoy the ritual aspect, may benefit from reading Donald Michael Kraig's book, *Modern Magick: Eleven Lessons in the High Magickal Arts*, which might be seen as a Cliff's Notes version of the lessons of the Hermetic order of the Golden Dawn.

To round out an education in the esoteric science of witchcraft, it is beneficial to have a mastery of other languages. Learning Latin, Greek, Hebrew or Old Norse enables you to have a deeper understanding of texts by being able to study them in their original language. Learning multiple languages, even modern ones, illuminates the etymology of words and helps you to make important connections. Furthermore, the study of ancient languages brings to light the fact that the official history of the world is highly flawed because ancient languages like Old Norse and Latin are so very highly sophisticated.

Much like official science and official medicine, official history seems designed to create an artificial narrative. Studying occult texts, historical events like the witchcraft trials and folk practices from Europe, the United States and around the world, illuminates the dark corners of world history and broadens your view of witchcraft and methods of spell casting.

The Basics: The Elements

The study of witchcraft and the occult is a life-long undertaking, but the most important knowledge a beginning spell caster should have is an understanding of the elements. The five elements of ether, fire, water, air, and earth are a central theme in esoteric texts because it is this portion of the cosmology, which, if understood and mastered, leads to success in manipulating events in the physical world of the common five senses.

These elements are the product of primordial forces and are the precursors to physical existence. It must be stressed, that they are not physical things, gods or beings and they are not to be worshiped. This is an important point for people who have been subjected to the mind control programming of Western religion. Such people should take caution along the course of their education not to fall into worship of any gods, spirits, gurus or historical figures.

The elements and other aspects of primordial creation are sometimes personified as a means of understanding and relating to them, but they are never gods, as such. They should be seen as forces, powers, energies or intelligences to be studied and worked with.

It is important to understand that in no case do the terms used to describe the elements refer to physical earth or the planet Earth, nor do the terms fire, water and air refer to actual fire, water and air. These terms are used as an expression of esoteric principles and not to be taken literally, just as the term "god" is not to be taken literally.

Consider the following definitions:

Five Elements: Akasha or ether; fire, water and earth. Akasha gave birth to the other four elements, the first being fire.

Akasha: An element of dynamic spirit; the quintessence.

Fire: The active element of the electrical force, which is characterized by heat and expansion.

Water: The opposite of fire, it is the receptive element of the electrical force. Its properties are coolness and contraction.

Air: A medium that provides an equilibrium between fire and water.

Earth: Formed by the union of fire, water and air, it is the most densely physical of the elements. It is the principle most closely related to physical existence.

The Kabbalistic name of "god" is the Tetragrammaton, Jod He Vau He, which is an expression of the last four of the aforementioned elements.

Because akasha is the parent of all four of the others, it naturally contains the seed of all four elements within it. Each element, also, contains a polarity of natures, which are sometimes described as repelling and attracting, light and dark, negative and positive, constructive and destructive or male and female.

SKILL

Esoteric science remains entirely theoretical to the novice until he or she experiences its principles through practical application. Along with developing your skills as a spell caster by working spells regularly and often, you can support this ability by developing a related skill set involving the healing arts, meditation, dowsing, divination and astrology.

Meditation helps to develop your focus and ability to concentrate even in adverse circumstances. It can, also, help you to develop a storage of personal power or life force energy, which you can use to empower your spells

The practice of the healing arts is one of the best ways to gain practical experience with the principles of esoteric science and see them at work. Applying herbalism, homeopathy, radionics and other types of healing based on the esoteric science of witchcraft. The best way to learn is to begin practicing. Acquire books and equipment to teach yourself or take classes in these subjects. Keep in mind the legal restraints in the U.S. and other countries on these practices.

Improve your psychic abilities by conducting your own parapsychological experiments at home, wither alone or with a partner. Examples of parapsychology tests involve the use of Zener cards, which contain a set of symbols, which can be applied a variety of ways to help you test and expand your psychic abilities. The Psychic Science web site (www.psychicscience.org) offers helpful and entertaining online parapsychology tests.

If you enjoy working with others and being part of a group, you may benefit from getting in touch with a variety of parapsychological and psychical research societies, such as the Parapsychological Association (www.parapsych.org); the American Society for Psychical Research (www.aspr.com); the International Association for Near-Death Studies (www.iands.org); and the Society for Psychical Research (www.spr.ac.uk).

Dowsing is another example of the practical application of the esoteric scientific theory of waves and the radiation of frequency of harmonics from objects. The human mind and body is a sensitive instrument and with the aide of a pendulum or dowsing rod, you can quickly develop your skills at intercepting and interpreting these fields. You can easily learn dowsing on your own with some practice. There are, also, two major organizations devoted to teaching people the art and science of dowsing, which you may find beneficial: The American Society of Dowsers (www.dowsers.org) and the British Society of Dowsers (www.britishdowsers.org).

Furthermore, learning about and developing a degree of mastery of astrology, the tarot and palmistry is a practical way to expand your skills and advance your knowledge of the esoteric science of witchcraft.

Pursue any of these subjects that interest you and you will soon find that the knowledge and skill you acquire will help you to become a more proficient spell caster.

Witchcraft Power Exercises for Charging Your Spells

Increasing your personal supply of life force energy is the key to making your spells work. When you conduct a spell, you use this energy to give strength to every aspect of the operation.

The objects used in spells should be charged with the four primary elemental forces: Fire; water; air and earth.

Again, when we speak of elements in this way, we are not referring to actual fire and water, but to esoteric concepts of forces that possess similar qualities. The terms, fire, air, water and earth, are not to be taken literally. While they are sometimes symbolically represented in spells or rituals, it is only to remind practitioners of these esoteric concepts and not to create a worship or reverence for physical nature.

The two main elements you must concern yourself with for the purpose of charging objects are fire and water. Within every atom and within you, two principle forces are at work, one is electric and fiery and the other is magnetic and watery in nature. These elements are called fire and water respectively and refer to the electromagnetic force within all of nature, including the metaphysical world. Here, again, nature does not refer to the great outdoors, but to the universal construct as a whole. It is these two elements that create a powerful force within you which you can direct in order to gather more energy and charge objects.

The two elementary forces, fire and water, are similar to the properties in a battery. One has a positive charge and the other one has a negative charge. This charge is not only electromagnetic, it is, also, has a wave form. The fiery principle repels and exerts force in an outward motion, whereas the watery principle, attracts and exerts a magnetizing force in an inward motion. This repelling and attracting, in and out motion is the nature of the electromagnetic force.

It is necessary for you to be able to quiet your mind and focus for just a few minutes at a time to charge an object. Relax yourself by taking a couple of deep breaths and releasing the tension from your body.

You may perform these exercises at any time in any position that is comfortable to you. Perform them regularly to increase your power.

Exercise No. 1
Exercise for Focus and Increased Life Force

Use this simple, but powerful exercise to improve your ability to focus your mind for short periods of time and increase your personal supply of life force energy.

Assume a comfortable position in a place where you can relax undisturbed for a few minutes.

1. Inhale very deeply to the count of 6

2. Retain this breath in your lungs for the count of 3

3. Exhale completely to the count of 6

4. Hold for the count of 3

5. Repeat the previous steps 10 to 15 times

You do not have to do this perfectly to benefit from it. It is ideal if you can breathe in through your nose and out through your mouth. If for some reason, you cannot do this, then breathe in and out through your mouth only.

Train yourself to focus on what you are doing while you are breathing and to think of nothing else for just the time it takes to do 10 to 15 repetitions. If a distracting thought comes into your mind during the course of your breathing, dismiss the idea by telling yourself you will think about it when you have finished your breathing exercise.

You will probably master this very quickly. If you can find the time to do this once or twice per day, your ability to focus your mind on one thing for a sustained period of time will increase.

Once you have successfully performed this several times, try incorporating a simple visualization exercise, as follows:

Use the same breathing pattern given above. This time, as you inhale, imagine that the air molecules you are drawing into your lungs are very dense so that they form a shimmering white light, tinged with a slightly blue hue. This fresh, vibrant energy is the electromagnetic life force from the etheric field. As you draw it in, every cell in your body is nourished and energized.

Upon each exhale, imagine that dirty, depleted energy is leaving your body. If you have an area of your body that is tense or where you are feeling any pain, focus your breathing on this part of your body. For example, if you have a pain in your right knee, as you exhale, see the depleted or damaged energy flowing out of it. Upon the inhale, see the fresh, vibrant, white-bluish energy coming into your right knee and energizing the cells of the body in that location.

Use this breathing exercise to increase your personal storage of life force energy. Use the same 6-3-6-3 breathing formula as before. But, this time keep all of the energy in your body and do not expel any upon exhale.

Inhale as before, visualizing the white-bluish energy coming into your body, but as you exhale, instead of seeing the energy go out with your breath, use your breath to further condense and push the energy into the cells of your body. Upon each repetition, you will see your body filling up with this vibrant energy, which becomes denser and more vibrant upon each inhale and exhale.

After you have done these breathing exercises for a little while, you will find that you can perform them while other things are going on around you. Distractions do not interfere with your ability to breathe or to manipulate the energy around you because you have greatly increased your ability to focus your mind.

Exercise No. 2
Akashic Meditation

The following meditation demonstrates how the elements come together to increase the power of the life force within you. Each time a witch performs this exercise, his or her personal power becomes a little stronger and more densely concentrated than before.

Assume your usual meditative posture, which may be sitting, standing or lying down. Visualize a black ball of energy tinged with purple that is popping and crackling like lightning in the pit of your stomach, located right on your spinal column, behind your navel. Remain conscious of your breathing. Upon each inhale, draw this energy in and with each exhale concentrate it into a dense ball in the pit of your stomach.

This ball of energy you are forming is comprised of pure akashic force. Continue to breathe and draw in the energy, compressing it into this vibrant ball. Breathe deeply and evenly. As you perform this exercise, you may be tempted to shorten your breath, but keep your focus and breathe deeply and deliberately.

The power to compress and concentrate the force is in the exhale. Weight lifters and bodybuilders will be very familiar with this principle because they know from experience that it is easier to exert force on an object while exhaling. Keep the same steady rhythm to your breathing as you would if you were lifting weights in the gym.

The seed of the other four elements resides within the akashic force. Therefore, once you have developed a sufficient supply of akasha within you, you will find it very easy to generate the four elements. The two most important of these are fire and water.

Exercise No. 3
Fire Meditation

After you have collected akashic energy and compressed it into a ball for a few minutes, begin drawing in the element of fire. This is an energy, dense enough to appear as a white mist tinged with red. By the same breathing method as before, draw it in and compress it into the ball for a few minutes.

Again, put your mental focus on the place inside your body located on your spine and behind your navel. With each breath, pull the element of fire, the active component of electromagnetic energy, out of the environment and form it into a little ball in the pit of your stomach.

Keep growing this energetic ball with each breath, which you will see as a ball of bright, white light, slightly tinged with a vibrant shade of red. Continue growing this ball and condensing its power until you have dense accumulation of it.

Exercise No. 4
Water Meditation

While holding the fiery ball from the previous meditation there in the pit of your stomach, begin to accumulate the water element from the environment around you. Add it to the existing dense ball.

This energy is tinged with blue and green and it swirls around like smoke as you gather it out of the air and pull it into the ball of energy. Do this until you have a more or less equal amount of fire and water element gathered together in this ball.

The air element exists naturally as a force of equilibrium between the elements of fire and water. You do not need to make a conscious effort to include it.

Exercise No. 5
Earth Meditation

After you have accumulated a dense ball of fire and water that you are satisfied with, draw in a little bit of earthy, dark brownish-red and gold energy to bring the vibratory level down just slightly. This helps to make the energy more dense and physical.

This is how you gather electromagnetic energy. Using your imagination, you can now cause the ball of energy to disperse and go down into the ground. Or, you may continue with the operation of charging.

Exercise No. 6
Releasing and Charging

Place before you the object you want to charge, whether it is a candle, a potion you have created, a glass of water, a talisman or any other object you might use in a spell.

Close your eyes for a moment and imagine the entire world as nothing more than a sea of vibrating energy. Become aware of the infinite matrix of tiny spinning atoms. Now, focus your attention on just one of these atoms and project your conscious awareness into the center of it. What you find there is an electromagnetic force, which is tinged by the nature of whatever thing it is a part of.

It is on this subatomic level that you will be projecting your energy into objects. These objects function as multidimensional holograms and like holograms, if you affect one part of it, you affect the entire thing.

You may open your eyes or keep them closed while charging an object. Hold the object to be charged or place your hands over and around it. In your mind, see this item on its atomic level as a collection of vibrating atoms. By the force of your will, cause the ball of energy you accumulated to move through your body, out of your hands and finger tips into the center of the atoms that comprise the object. Alternatively, you may project it straight out of your abdomen by means of a visualization in which it simply pours directly out of you and fills the form of the object before you.

Once this is done, the object is energized with the electromagnetic elements of fire and water. You must now project your mental powers upon the energy in the object and impregnate it with your will or intention.

Suppose, for example, that you want to charge a candle, which you plan to burn as part of a spell. As we will see in the next chapter, the smoke from this candle, which is its essence, will be carried into the outer environment to impregnate the energy around it with your desires.

Begin by filling yourself with energy as previously instructed. Then, direct the accumulated energy into the object. With your mind's eye, see the energy filling first one atom, then every atom of the candle. Once you have filled the object completely, impress your desires upon the vibrating force you have placed within it.

You may do this by speaking to the object as if it were a person. Say, "Now, you shall become an instrument for my will. You are to find and return to me the money and wealth that I desire." You may, also, use a formal incantation or only the force of your thoughts.

Once you have done this, you may end with the word, "Amen," or the phrase, "So mote it be," or whatever words of power you might want to add to this procedure. Your object is now fully charged with your focused energy and impregnated with your intention by the force of your will.

SPIRITUAL AIDE

A body of research by the Spiritualists and their offshoot, the Spiritists, supplies a great deal of information about the world beyond the physical, although it fails to entirely illuminate the nature of the spirit world. It is not entirely certain if spirits are something that comes from within the mind of a person or if they are external intelligences. But, for the purpose of casting spells, this difference is of less importance than the actual results achieved by means of enlisting aide from a variety of different categories of spirits.

It is by means of spiritual assistance that many of the most remarkable feats in witchcraft can be achieved. This assistance is obtained by establishing long-term relationship with a spirit who has the particular abilities required by your work.

The matter of how people interface with spirits and which ones they communicate with is a very personal one. Methods range from the fairly simple ones of the trance mediums of the spiritualists to the absurd complexities of ceremonial magicians.

The development of spiritual mediumship abilities is one means of establishing a relationship with spirits, however, these spirits provide information more often than assistance. But, it is possible to develop a relationship with spirit assistants without becoming bogged down in complex and often useless rituals.

For instance, the enlistment of saints for spiritual assistance and as natural manipulators of the elements or the "god force" is typical of witchcraft practices in Catholic countries. The Catholic saints and the folk saints of Catholic nations are often spirits of the dead or very powerful ancient spirits or thought forms that can perform a variety of tasks according to their nature. But, anyone who takes the time to understand the nature of a saint and to work with that spirit can establish a relationship with it and employ it.

Angels, fallen angels and demons are described in terms of their abilities and their orders or hierarchy. There are innumerable systems of these spirits, some of whom may be contacted only at certain hours and even certain minutes of the day. Once contact has been established an agreement or pact can be made to easily obtain the services of the spirit at will at any time in the future.

The power of the hereditary witch lies not only in the base of knowledge and skill passed from one generation to the next, but in the inheritance of domestic spirits or familiars. These spirits are fed and grow stronger from one generation to the next and aide the witch in spell casting and all manner of other operations.

Again, the caveat for those who have been in contact with Christian religion: Be careful not to fall into worship of spirits, but communicate and work with these intelligences. Spirits are servants and sometimes friends, but they are never idols or gods from whom to take orders.

Ultimately, the power to make a spell work is in the spell caster. It is derived from his or her knowledge base, skill and ability to generate energy and, in some cases, enlist external forces. The degree to which any procedure will be successful depends on the knowledge, skill, ability and power of the individual witch.

If you feel an operation needs more power, ask for help from a like-minded person with the same goal. For instance, if you are a member of a coven or work closely with another witch whom you trust, then ask for his or her assistance.

When this is lacking, as it is more often than not, then ask for help from spirits. Solitary witches rely on well-established relationships with spirits to intercede for them and to empower their workings. The dead are as much friends as the living, when you cultivate a relationship with them.

The author goes into greater detail on how to contact and work with spirits in the book, *Practical Black Magic: How to Hex and Curse Your Enemies*. Franz Bardon's book, *Magical Evocation*, gives practical information for contacting and working with spiritual assistants who perform a wide variety of tasks.

Prayer and Incantation

According to Eli Buriss in the book, *Taboo, Magic, Spirits: A Study of Primitive Elements in Roman Religion*, Christian prayer evolved from incantation in Rome. The two are similar except that incantation doesn't always involve a request to a spirit.[11]

Both prayers and incantations are often repeated during the casting of a spell. Prayers and incantations may or may not rhyme and they may be made in either the form of a request or a command to spirits or elemental forces. Both are used to find resonance with intelligences or forces and direct the flow of energy in an operation.

Classic prayers and incantations like the Our Father or the Carmen Arvale may be used or new ones may be invented. Elemental forces, spirits words of power or names of god may be incorporated to give strength to a working.

Magical alphabets and runes are another means of adding power to and directing the energy of a spell, which are similar to prayers or incantations, except they are written or inscribed.

The Elder Futhark or the Old Norse Runes are spells themselves, when they are properly arranged and their power is invoked. Their use is described by Edred Thorsson in *Futhark: A Handbook of Rune Magic*, which is a translation of some ancient Icelandic documents.

Each letter of the Hebrew alphabet, also, has specific attributes, symbolically, numerologically and Kabbalistically, which can be used to add power to spells.

Some magical alphabets, such as the Runes of Honorious, are of a more dubious origin, but are nonetheless powerful in a working. These runes are attributed to Honorius of Thebes, but were first published in *Johannes Trithemius' Polygraphia* in 1581. To use them, substitute a rune for the sounds in the words of your prayer or incantation.

Traditionally, it is acknowledged that secrecy enhances the power of a spell. If nothing else, it prevents another witch from commandeering your operation by tapping into the energy you have put into it.

For spells and incantations you commonly use, you may create shortcuts. These are signals or gestures you assign to them. An example of a well-known shortcut is the making of the sign of the cross by Catholics. This is an instantaneous invocation of the powers of the Tetragrammaton or the power of "god," including the four elements and the akashic force. The hands in prayer with the palms together and fingertips touching creates an energetic circuit and helps the body to fill up very quickly with elemental powers required to charge the items in a spell.

You may devise and assign your own unique finger or hand signals, which might include tapping fingers together in a specific manner or even uttering a single word, which is a shortcut to longer prayers, invocations or incantations.

Questions

1. Which of the witch's skills is the most important one to practice because it demonstrates most visibly the esoteric science behind witchcraft and spell casting?

2. What are the two main ways to empower your spells?

3. Name the five elements.

4. Which element contains the seed of all of the others?

5. Which two elements are the most important ones for charging the objects in your spells?

6. Which element is associated with the active principle and vigorous action?

7. Which element is associated with the receptive principle and magnetism?

8. Which element is the medium that provides the equilibrium between fire and water?

9. Which element is closest the physical plane or density?

10. In the Akashic Meditation, which is used to increase your vital energy supply, what are the two colors associated with the akashic field?

Answers

1. The healing arts, in particular, homeopathy and radionics.

2. By means of your own internal life force power and by means of spiritual assistance.

3. Akasha (sometimes called ether or the quintessence), fire, water, air and earth.

4. Akasha

5. Fire and water

6. Fire

7. Water

8. Air

9. Earth

10. Black and purple

FINAL STEP: METHODS OF RELEASING ENERGY

The final step of every spell involves the release of directed energy. This last step is important because once a spell has been performed, if the energy involved is held onto by the spell caster, it will never have the opportunity to work. It must be released upon the object of your spell and into the outer environment to influence the universal vibrational field.

The release of energy often involves placing items from the spell in a certain location and leaving it there. Once a spell is performed, the complete release of its energy is accomplished by the spell caster afterward forgetting about the entire issue.

The act of placing an object in a certain place and then forgetting about has a two-fold purpose in witchcraft because it not only releases the energy, but provides some psychological assistance to the spell caster. Burying an item, burning it or throwing it somewhere and returning home without looking back are examples of this. Not only is the spell item placed somewhere to disperse its influence, but the spell caster makes a mental and emotional break from the situation by means of this act.

In many spells the energy is released through burning and allowing the essence of the charge to be carried through the air, liquid being poured out into the earth, or an object being buried or hidden away, although there are many other methods you can employ based on your purpose. It may, also, be left in a particular place to exert its influence slowly and steadily upon a person or place.

Take care, especially with this final step of spell casting, not to violate any laws by committing an act that might be construed as littering, trespassing, attempted poisoning or improper usage of the postal service. You should conduct your spells subtly, secretly and without running up against the law. Another reason for secrecy is so that the spells are not discovered and their influence removed by the affected party should they become suspicious.

Earth

One of the most common methods of releasing the energy of a spell involves burial in the earth. An item is buried in different kinds of places depending on how you wish to release its influence or, in some cases, neutralize it.

Objects are sometimes placed in a container such as a box, bag or bottle or wrapped in foil before this is done. If the idea is to preserve this energy in a particular place so that it continues to influence that area, the container should be of a more sturdy and durable nature.

If the influence of a spell is intended for a person, the object should be buried near or at the person's property. If your intention is to sow discord in this person's home, bury the object in their backyard. If it is intended to cause financial problems, bury it in the front yard. If you wish to destroy the person's business, bury the object near or at their business or place of employment.

Burying an object beneath the doorstep of a home imparts its influence, whether for good or evil, to the members of the household and all who must pass over it as they enter. For example, the classic witch's bottle is buried beneath the doorstep of the home to disperse its protective influence. The refuse from spells for peace and prosperity are commonly buried at or near the threshold to disseminate their influences to the entire house.

The liquids of spells and rituals are sometimes poured into the earth as a libation or an offering to earth spirits and to obtain their assistance.

The remains of rituals, such as candle wax and ashes, which may be of a benevolent or malefic nature should be disposed of accordingly. Never bury the remains of any malefic working on your property or keep it in your home.

Cemeteries

Bury spell items in a graveyard to cause serious illness, insanity and death. The items may be contained in a box, a wax coffin a bag or an animal skull. Items from malefic spells and rituals can be safely disposed of in a cemetery to neutralize their effects, as well.

Graveyard burials are, also, employed to obtain help from the spirits of the dead in any matter. In this instance, it is important to establish a relationship with these spirits.

In American Hoodoo certain protocols are observed with regard to cemeteries, which are the homes of spirits. Usually, one or more spirits act as guardians and they must be acknowledged if the working is to be successful. Always behave respectfully in a cemetery. Ask permission to enter at the gate and leave a few coins as payment to the spirits. Ask them for their assistance, always leaving some sort of payment or gift for them, such as coins or flowers, in return.

If you are concerned about being harmed or followed by the spirits of a cemetery or if you are entering to perform malefic witchcraft, enter the gate walking backward. Depart the cemetery through the same gate by which you entered. Thank the spirits for their assistance without turning to look back. If you are still concerned about being followed, cross over a river, stream or a crossroad on your way home.

In the American witchcraft tradition of the Ozark Mountains, cemeteries are places inhabited not only by the spirits of the dead, but by "the devil" and it is here that he is met and powers and assistance are obtained from him.

Crossroads

A crossroad naturally manifests the power of the four directions and the five elements, the fifth element being symbolized by the point in the center at which the four roads meet.

Spell items that contain unwholesome energy may be safely disposed of at a crossroad. It is customary to toss, bury or otherwise leave it at a crossroad, then turn and go home without ever turning to look behind you. This act symbolizes the total release of energy. To rid yourself of an influence, go on a Saturday during a Waning Moon and bury the object.

Crossroads are, also, places to confuse an enemy. To confound evil spirits or evil people, leave the items from a spell at a crossroad far from your home.

Conversely, leaving items from a spell at a series of crossroads is a method of linking people or places together. Influences can be driven away from a person or place by leaving remnants from a spell at a series of crossroads, thereby driving the influence in some other direction.

Leaving an item at a crossroad as an offering is a way to obtain the assistance of crossroad spirits like Hecate (who governs three-way crossroads), Santa Muerte, San Simon of Guatemala, Eshu, Eleggua, Papa Legba, Lord Shiva and Lord Ganesha.

Spirits of the crossroads, including those called "the devil" or "the blackman" are, also, sources of power, knowledge and assistance in other matters. In the Ozarks, pacts with such spirits are made at crossroads by waiting for the spirit's arrival on nine consecutive nights.

Crossroads are the place for disposal of ritual items and charms related to road opener spells, which are spells that affect the abstract outer environment and remove obstacles from the path to success in any endeavor.

Trees

As living things, trees have the power to absorb and transfer energy to nearby dwellings and passers by.

The location of the tree is important. Familiar trees in a front yard may be endowed with protective or fortunate influences by means of a charm hidden in a hollow, dangled from a branch or buried near its roots. For example, spirit balls are pretty glass charms, which are hung from the branches of nearby trees to trap malefic spirits and prevent them from entering a home.

Trees are, also, used in the dark arts, to hide the influence of a spell and allow it to keep working against the person who dwells near the tree.

Trees in a cemetery, especially old and gnarled trees have a dark influence. Items intended to cause harm and destruction may be buried beneath the roots of such trees or hidden in its natural hollows.

The species of tree may, also, be relevant to your purpose. For example, items from spells revolving around the theme of love may be well-disposed of in an apple tree on or near the property of the object of the spell. If the spell involves money, a Malabar chestnut tree might be used. To increase the power of prophesy or clairvoyance, a willow or yew tree might be employed. A list of trees and their metaphysical associations is provided in the *Appendix*.

Fire

Burning is commonly used to completely destroy something or someone. Effigies of people are burned piece by piece to cause the wasting away and destruction of a person a little at a time. Burning is, also, a way to destroy the influence of objects, especially those used in malefic spells.

Petition papers used in spells and rituals are often burned to disseminate their influence by smoke. The ashes may then be buried according to the nature of their influence.

Burning incense, candles and old-fashioned oil lamps is a means of making an offering to helpful spirits and releasing influences into the environment. The smoke of a fire is used to carry messages to spirits of the dead and the living.

Water

Sinking spell items in water is a method used to cause an enemy's business, health or relationships to fail as the item takes in more water.

Items are disposed of in running water, such as a river or stream, to carry their influence far away. This is common in banishing spells. Influences may be sent away on water by means of flushing them down the toilet or allowing them to flow down the drain.

Some dark arts spells, harness the power of the tides by floating an item containing influences upon a victim in water that rises and falls, which means that the influence of the spell will rise and fall with the tides or the waxing and waning of the moon. For example, if the bewitched is to suffer from a chronic illness, it will worsen with the rising tide in a cyclical fashion. By this means a victim may be caused to suffer from mental conditions like manic depression and severe mood swings.

Boiling items in water releases the their influences into the air by means of steam, either to create an abstract influence on the environment or to influence a particular person.

Wells and natural bodies of water like lakes, ponds and oceans are places to make offerings to water spirits and obtain their assistance for a working.

Water that has been used as an offering to spirits should be disposed of according to its influence. If it was used for a negative working, it can be thrown at a crossroad or flushed down a toilet or drain. If it contains vibrations you want to keep near you, use it to water a houseplant or pour it just outside your doorstep.

Air

To cast an abstract influence into the general environment, blow the powder from a spell in the directions of the four winds or the four cardinal points. For example, a Hoodoo powder formula empowered by a spell which is intended to improve finances or attract love and success of a general nature may be blown into the air to disperse its influence upon the cosmos.

Finely ground powders are released upon the air by blowing them in the direction of the person or thing you want to influence. This is another way to release the influence of a spell whenever the items involved have been reduced to ashes.

Steam carries influences by a combination of water and air; smoke disperses them by means of fire and air.

Animals and Insects

Winged creatures, including birds and insects, are spiritual messengers. Insects have a strong relationship to the spirit world and are used as a means of releasing the influence of a spell. They may be employed to cause insanity, decay and destruction or to bring good luck and happy influences.

Animals, especially pets, are sometimes used as vehicles for transferring energy from a spell and releasing it upon another person. Whatever energy is imparted to the animal can be conveyed to the next person it comes in contact with.

Here, again, it is important to be careful for the sake of safety, especially that of the animal. Potions with perfumes and oils should not be applied to the fur of animals, especially cats. It is sufficient to apply a small amount of powder to your hands before touching the animal with the intention of transferring this energy. A pet's collar may be passed through the smoke of incense to imbue it with the desired energy before sending it back to its owner to whom this energy is to be ultimately imparted.

Insects are kept and fed, then their spirits are employed in various ways. For example, an insect my be released into the environment to do harm to an enemy. Sugar and syrup are used to attract ants to an Passive Substitution to cause insanity and death.

Direct Contact

If you have access to the person or place upon which a spell is to have its influence, you may accomplish the final release of your working by means of direct contact. This should always be done secretly and mindfully of the laws where you live. If you are unable to release the spell without violating a law or directly endangering yourself or someone else, then you should use an alternative method.

Historically, the influence of a spell is delivered by means of food or drink, which is why witches once had a reputation as poisoners. Some potions are intended to be consumed, thus releasing the influence of a spell directly upon the person. If you choose to use this method, never put a harmful agent into someone's food or drink.

Another probably far safer method of bringing a person in direct contact is by administering a potion or other magical substance to the person's clothing or shoes. If you, the spell caster, are the subject of your own spell, then you will have a good idea about the safety of applying a potion directly to yourself. For safety's sake, take special care applying potions to others.

Potions are sometimes sent directly to a person in an envelope. Take caution using the postal service for such an endeavor as it could be misconstrued and may be a serious violation of the law. Historically, spell casters send an envelope containing a magical powder or a paper secretly anointed with a potion to bring the subject of the spell in direct contact with the substance, thereby transferring its influence.

Anointing door knobs the person must touch with oil or administering powder to them is another method of direct contact.

The spell may be released by placing a magical substance in a place where the object of the spell must walk through it. Retroactively, this is done by means of "foot track" magic in which you take the dirt from the person's foot print and apply the potion to it, thus releasing its influence upon the person.

Energy may be transferred to a person or place by giving an object of influence away as a gift or leaving it somewhere to be found. The objects in the spell can be decorated or combined with money or some attractive object and left for a person to find, thereby transferring its influence by means of direct contact. The person may even be inclined to carry an attractive "gift" with them or bring it into their home or place of business where it will release its influence for good or evil.

House washes are another example of the deployment of influences directly inside a home or place of business, usually to repel bad people or bad luck and attract desirable people and good fortune.

Charms and Talismans

Charms and talismans are a common method of imparting the influence of a spell to one's self or to someone who is the subject of a benevolent working. Charms carried close to the skin, either pinned inside clothing or placed inside undergarments or in a pocket.

Some charms are related to spirits that must be invoked once to obtain their power. Others, like mojo bags, are charged regularly to keep their energy strong. Then, it is carried with you to disseminate its influence on you and your environment.

Place a charm or other items from spells wherever you want to disperse their influence. For example, money drawing charms may be kept in a purse, wallet, safe or the company cash register. Keep protective charms in your vehicle, around the house and yard. Place charms to keep out evil spirits and bad people in doorways, windows, chimneys and virtually any possible entry way including water pipes. Charms to protect property may be buried at the four cardinal points, buried under the hearth or doorstep of the property or deployed in trees.

The witch's bottle or Bellarmine bottle is a historical example of a protective charm which is commonly buried upside down beneath the doorstep or the foundation of a house to protect the person who lives there. It protects against malefic witchcraft and its contents are comprised of a person's own urine and hair boiled, then placed in a bottle along with needles, nails and other items.

Needles with broken eyes stuck in doors and bewitched blades placed in window sashes are examples of protective charms placed at the exact location where their defensive influence is to be released.

Other Methods

When it is not practical or desirable to bury items from beneficial spells, the objects may be hidden inside a home or business to disseminate their influence. They may be sewn inside mattresses or pillowcases, placed inside closets and drawers and even inside walls, floors and household furnishings.

A common method of releasing a spell, especially a love or domination spell, is to place an item beneath the person's bed. This location is, also, used to release the influence of destructive spells and those intended to drive away enemies.

Geometrically fix the items from a spell within or near your home by placing the item of influence within the center of a cross pattern. This arrangement symbolizes the five elements and it is sometimes called a "five spot" because the arrangement resembles a playing card in the denomination of five. It is generally placed secretly within the home. For example, a potion may be administered at the four points of the cross, with a Passive Substitution placed at the center of it. This is a permanent arrangement that is hidden in the house under a bed, a rug, furniture and more traditionally under floorboards. As long as the object remains in place, the influence of the spell will continue to be dispersed.

Generally speaking, releasing an item from a spell into the ground is a method of invoking the aid of earth spirits; releasing it upon the air may be an invocation to air spirits; placing it in a body of water may be an invocation to spirits of water; and burning it may be used as a means of connecting with spirits of fire to do your bidding.

Questions

1. At what location should you never bury the items from a dark arts spell?

2. Items from malefic witchcraft spells are buried in cemeteries to cause which of the following:

   A. Illness and death
   B. Health and well-being
   C. Financial improvement
   D. Love attraction

3. To completely destroy an object or its influence, subject it to which of the following:

   A. Earth
   B. Air
   C. Fire
   D. Water

4. To confuse an enemy, bury the object of a spell at:

   A. The base of a tree
   B. In your backyard
   C. In your enemy's backyard
   D. At a crossroad

5. To keep the influence of a spell close to you, bury it:

   A. In your backyard
   B. In your friend's backyard
   C. In a cemetery
   D. At a crossroad

6. Where should you put an item from a spell when you want to cause its influence to move away from you:

   A. Lake or pond
   B. River or stream
   C. A fire
   D. A tree

7. To cause the influence of a spell to wax and wane with the moon, you should do which of the following:

    A. Begin on the night of a Full Moon
    B. Float the item from the spell where the tides rise and fall
    C. Bury the item from the spell at a crossroad
    D. Burn the item and scatter the ashes on the wind

8. True or False? The following are examples of releasing a spell by means of direct contact: Applying a potion to a person's clothing; applying a magical substance to a doorknob at the person's office and presenting an item as a gift.

9. Place a charm or talisman wherever you want its influence to be worked most strongly. For example, which of the following would be the best place to put a money drawing charm?

    A. Your purse, wallet or cash register
    B. Your shoe
    C. Beneath your bed
    D. In the hollow of a tree in your yard

10. True or False? When the burial of items from malefic spells is not practical or desirable, the objects may be hidden inside your own home or business to disseminate their influence.

Answers

1. Never bury the items from a malefic spell on your own property.

2. A. Illness and death

3. C. Fire

4. D. Crossroad

5. A. In your backyard

6. B. River or stream

7. B. Float the item from the spell where the tides rise and fall

8. True

9. A. Your purse, wallet or cash register

10. False. Items from malefic or dark arts spells should never be kept in your own home or place of business.

LESSONS IN SPELL CASTING

In determining what kind of spell to use, consider the degree of access you have to the object of the spell. Other limitations may include what items you have at your disposal and what degree of access to or knowledge you have of the target of the spell.

Also, consider your own skill level. Highly trained magicians can act upon a subject at a distance with very little in the way of energetic substitutions. Although, using them can certainly make the task easier.

The following are examples of spells that involve situations in which the object of the spell is both known and unknown to you; they include concrete situations and abstract ones; and situations which varying amounts of information is available about the person or institution involved. Study these examples, then use the template below them to construct your own spells using the information in the previous chapters and the information provided in the *Appendix*.

Examples of Spells

These examples focus on the banishing of unwanted influences and protection from evil. These types of spells are the groundwork for the general practice of witchcraft. We will use previously discussed concepts and items referenced in the *Appendix* in these examples. With each spell, we will consider the following steps:

Step 1. Timing: Day or Planetary Hour; Moon Phase and Moon Sign

Step 2. Passive Substitution: That which represents the object of your spell; may be concrete or abstract

Step 3. Active Substitution: Potion; Zoological Effect or other agent

Step 4. Imitative Action: An action the represents your desire

Step 5. Colors

Step 6. Charging, which may include incantation or spiritual assistance

Step 7. Release

Banishing Spell Involving a Person Known to You

Scenario: You are bothered by a person who does not present a threat to your safety, but is an annoying pest who shows up at your home unannounced or calls you at inopportune times. This person is very familiar to you and you have previously considered him or her a friend, but you now wish to protect yourself from any further intrusions without causing them any harm. In this instance, you want to protect yourself from a particular person and ward off their influence. So, you should conduct a banishing spell.

Step 1. Choose beneficial timing by referring to the information in *Chapter 4*. The day, Saturday or the planetary hour of Saturn; during the Waning Moon and when the moon is in Scorpio or Capricorn are propitious times for performing banishing spells.

Step 2. Consult *Chapter 3*, which deals with sympathetic magic, including substitutions, actions and colors that may be employed. You may choose a Passive Substitution for this spell that involves Personal Effects since you know this person and may have access to hairs from the person's hair brush, a photograph or an item that contains the person's bodily fluids. Include these items in an effigy and baptize it in the name of the person.

Step 3. Choose an Active Substitution that reflects the action you wish to take upon the person. After consulting the list of potions in the *Appendix*, you decide that the best option is a Banishing potion.

Step 4. To apply Imitative Action tie the hands and feet and tape the mouth of the Passive Substitution that represents the pest.

Step 5. Consulting the list of colors and their associations in *Chapter 3*, it appears that the best color to use for candles and altar dressings is black.

Step 6. Charge this spell by means of the meditations described in *Chapter 5*. Impregnate the charge you have placed in the object with the force of your will. If you choose, use an incantation to direct this energy. Your incantation may be as simple as "[Name], go away; far away stay, forever and a day." Write a petition or request and place it under the candle or inscribe it on the side of the candle along with the name of the person to be banished.

Step 7. Release the power of this spell by applying the charged items to the effigy over the course of an odd number of days. Then, you may bury the object at a crossroad for an odd number of days before tossing it into a body of moving water. If you have direct access to the person, apply the potion you charged during this spell to something with which the object of this spell is likely to come in contact with, such as your door knob or your doorbell.

Banishing Spell Involving Unknown People

Scenario: You are bothered by unwanted contact with people you do not know, cannot identify and have no direct access to.

Step 1. Use the same timing as for the spell above.

Step 2. In this instance, you do not know the identity of the people who are bothering you, therefore, you will act upon the abstract.

Step 3. After consulting the *Appendix*, you decide to use a Zoological Substitution that represents pests: Flies.

Step 4. Employ Imitative Action by capturing the flies in a container and holding them captive until they die. Then burn their corpses to ashes to create a potion.

Step 5. Just as in the previous spell, use black as the color for your candles and altar items.

Step 6. Charge all of the objects in the spell. Recite an incantation, such as, "I banish all you bothers and pests; you are all unwanted guests; I banish you from my door; here, now and forever more."

Step 7. Blow the ashes upon the wind to impart their influence upon the cosmos or apply them to affected objects. For instance, if you are having a problem with unwanted visitors at your door, sprinkle the ashes on your porch. If you are receiving unwanted correspondence, sprinkle them inside your mail box. If you are receiving unwanted telephone calls, apply them to your telephone.

Spell Invoking Spiritual Assistance to Create a Protective Charm

Scenario: You are feeling harassed and bothered and you need general protection from pesky people, either known or unknown to you, and evil influences. You may choose any protective spirit to work with whom you have some rapport, this may be an ancestor, a spirit from the grave, a saint, a pagan god or animal spirit. In this example, a statue of the Mexican folk saint, Santa Muerte or Holy Death, is employed.

Step 1. Since this is a spell for general protection, begin your work on a Monday or during the planetary hour of the moon or, for more aggressive protection, on a Tuesday or the planetary hour of Mars; during a Full Moon or when the moon is in Libra for justice and harmony.

Step 2. Use your own Personal Effects, such as a few hairs, a blood spot, a photograph of yourself or nail clippings.

Step 3. Choose a protective potion from the *Appendix*, such as Fiery Wall of Protection, use Graveyard Dirt in a red mojo bag or use a Zoological Effect, such as the rattle of a rattlesnake. Place this item upon your altar to be charged by the spirit.

Step 4. Apply Imitative Action to this spell by placing your Personal Effects under the base of your Santa Muerte statue to show that you are under her protection.

Step 5. Use white for this spell if your goal is general protection. In this case, the candle color, your altar cloth and your Santa Muerte statue should be white. You may offer the Santa Muerte white roses, as well, to symbolize your request for protection, peace and harmony. For stronger protection, choose a black image of Santa Muerte and use a black candle.

Step 6. Charge the objects by asking for the assistance of Santa Muerte and the use of her power to protect you from all evil. In this case, it is customary to pray the Our Father prayer (See Glossary) three times to open and close your invocation. Write your request upon a petition paper and incorporate it into your prayer. After you have verbally made your request for protection to the spirit, place the petition paper beneath the candle or if it is small, you may wrap it around her scythe to symbolize her execution of your request.

Write your petition on the paper. The following example is very general, your own petition should be as specific to your situation as possible: "Let there be peace and harmony in my home and my work place. Let my home be untroubled by unwanted guests and visitors. Let my enemies forget about me and let any of them who try to find me lose their way."

Say a prayer to Santa Muerte, inserting the above petition, as follows:

O Most Holy Death who is most dear to my heart, who is my friend, who never leaves my side. I ask that you cloak me with the mantle of your protection. Allow me to overcome all obstacles and barriers, so that nothing is impossible for me. Destroy my enemies, both great and small, bring those who oppose me under my feet like meek lambs. Let me be victorious in all of my struggles and succeed in all my endeavors. I especially ask that you [Insert your petition]. In the name of the Father, the Son and the Holy Ghost. Amen.

Step 7. Allow the candle to burn down, make the sign of the cross and say three Glory Be prayers (See Glossary) over the items. Then, take the refuse from the candle and petition and bury it near your threshold or keep it in a drawer in your home where it will not be touched, so that the influence of this spell is kept close to you. Place the charged item from Step 3. into mojo bag and carry it with you to absorb its protective influence.

Template to Write a Spell for Any Purpose

Following the previous examples, design your own spells for the scenarios provided below. You will recall the following steps:

Step 1. Timing: Day or Planetary Hour; Moon Phase and Moon Sign
Step 2. Passive Substitution: That which represents the object of your spell; may be concrete or abstract
Step 3. Active Substitution: Potion; Zoological Effect or other agent
Step 4. Imitative Action: An action the represents your desire
Step 5. Colors
Step 6. Charging, which may include incantation or spiritual assistance
Step 7. Release

Lesson 1.
Love Spell

Scenario: You are attracted to someone at your school or place of employment with whom you have little contact outside the cafeteria. Therefore, you have limited access to this person, although you may be able to secretly obtain a photograph or an item with their bodily fluids on it such as a napkin or fork. You have no personal information about the object of your desire.

Step 1. Choose auspicious timing for a love attraction spell.
Step 2. Obtain a Personal Effect belonging to the object of your love
Step 3. Choose an Active Substitution
Step 4. Devise an Imitative Action
Step 5. Choose the appropriate color or colors
Step 6. Charge your spell
Step 7. Release the energy from your spell

Lesson 2.
Prosperity Spell

Scenario: You would like to increase the flow of abundance and wealth to yourself.

Step 1. Choose auspicious timing for a prosperity spell
Step 2. Choose a candle in a shape that is related to prosperity to be an abstract Passive Substitution
Step 3. Choose a relevant potion
Step 4. Devise an Imitative Action
Step 5. Choose the appropriate color or colors
Step 6. Charge your spell items
Step 7. Release the energy from your spell

Lesson 3.
Spell to Increase Physical Strength and Determination

Scenario: Lately, you have been feeling a little weak, both physically and mentally, and you wish to renew your strength and fortify your will.

Step 1. Choose auspicious timing.
Step 2. Choose a Passive Substitution to symbolize the abstract concept of physical strength and determination
Step 3. Choose an Active Substitution
Step 4. Optionally, devise an Imitative Action
Step 5. Choose the appropriate color or colors
Step 6. Charge your spell; optionally, write an incantation or choose a spirit to empower your work
Step 7. Release the energy from your spell

Lesson 4.
Spell to Ace a Test

Scenario: In order to advance to the next level at school or work, you must do very well on an upcoming test.

Step 1. Choose auspicious timing for success in education or career
Step 2. Choose a Passive Substitution that represents the test
Step 3. Choose an Active Substitution to represent your success
Step 4. Devise an Imitative Action to show your dominance in this matter
Step 5. Choose the appropriate color or colors
Step 6. Charge your spell
Step 7. Release the energy from your spell

Lesson 5.
Spell to Win at Poker

Scenario: You are an avid poker player who has been on a losing streak and you want to turn your luck around.

Step 1. Choose auspicious timing
Step 2. Obtain a Passive Substitution to represent your win
Step 3. Choose an Active Substitution
Step 4. Devise an Imitative Action
Step 5. Choose the appropriate color or colors
Step 6. Charge your spell
Step 7. Release the energy from your spell

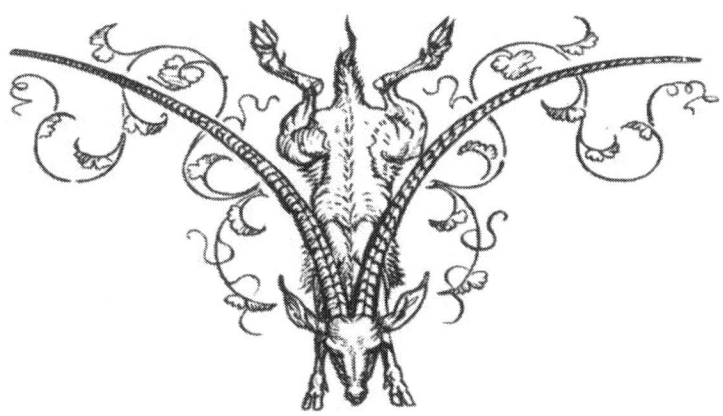

Lesson 6.
Spell to Stop Neighbors from Gossiping

Scenario: Your neighbors have started talking behind your back, whether what they are saying is the truth or not, it is interfering with your life and you want them to stop right away.

Step 1. Choose auspicious timing
Step 2. Obtain a Passive Substitution to represent your neighbors or the problem
Step 3. Choose an Active Substitution
Step 4. Devise an Imitative Action
Step 5. Choose the appropriate color or colors
Step 6. Charge your spell
Step 7. Release the energy from your spell

Lesson 7.
Spell to Gain the Admiration and Approval of Others

Scenario: You would like to gain more influence at your workplace, school or social club by increasing your popularity.

Step 1. Choose auspicious timing
Step 2. Obtain a Passive Substitution to represent yourself in this situation
Step 3. Choose an Active Substitution
Step 4. Devise an Imitative Action
Step 5. Choose the appropriate color or colors
Step 6. Charge your spell
Step 7. Release the energy from your spell

Lesson 8.
Spell to Break an Emotional Attachment

Scenario: You have been betrayed by a lifelong friend and have severed your relationship with that person. Nonetheless, you still harbor sympathetic feelings for your old friend, which you would like to be rid of.

Step 1. Choose auspicious timing
Step 2. Obtain a Passive Substitution to represent the parties involved
Step 3. Choose an Active Substitution
Step 4. Devise an Imitative Action
Step 5. Choose the appropriate color or colors
Step 6. Charge your spell
Step 7. Release the energy from your spell

Lesson 9.
Protection Spell for Your Car

Scenario: You have a new job that requires you to drive your car on dangerous freeways and park it in high crime areas.

Step 1. Choose auspicious timing
Step 2. Obtain a Passive Substitution to represent your car
Step 3. Choose an Active Substitution
Step 4. Devise an Imitative Action
Step 5. Choose the appropriate color or colors
Step 6. Charge your spell
Step 7. Release the energy from your spell

Lesson 10.
Spell to Get Someone to Sign a Divorce Agreement

Scenario: You are presenting your spouse with divorce papers, which you want him or her to sign, although the terms of the agreement are not in his or her favor.

Step 1. Choose auspicious timing
Step 2. Obtain a Passive Substitution
Step 3. Choose an Active Substitution
Step 4. Devise an Imitative Action
Step 5. Choose the appropriate color or colors
Step 6. Charge your spell
Step 7. Release the energy from your spell

Solutions to the Lessons

The following are only suggested solutions to applying the spell casting template. They are by no means the only correct answers, but rather a guide because the possibilities are endless and limited only to your own research, creativity and inspiration.

Lesson 1
Love Spell

Step 1. Friday (or planetary hour of Venus) for love; Tuesday (or planetary hour of Mars) for passion. Any moon phase but the Waning Moon is a good time for this spell. Choose the New Moon for a new love affair or the Waxing or Full Moon for love attraction. Conduct the spell when the Moon is in Taurus for love attraction; the Moon in Scorpio for an affair of a more sexual nature and the Moon in Cancer if your objective involves a long-term relationship or matrimony.

Step 2. Personal effects: Photo, a signature, something worn by the person, especially unlaundered underwear, or something with saliva or other bodily fluids on it. This item may be combined with the candle above, in which the candle will become part of the Passive Substitution in this spell. Or, you may use the Personal Effects as a stand alone Passive Substitution. Alternatively, you may place these items in a cloth or wax effigy of the person, which you have named and baptized for the person. A figure candle of the appropriate color and gender for this spell may be used as part of your Passive Substitution, especially if you inscribe his or her name on the side of it and place the Personal Effects in a hollow in the bottom.

You may, also, use your own Personal Effects in this spell and designate a candle to represent yourself.

Step 3. Choose a potion such as Love and Lust or Love Attraction. Empower it by adding your own blood or sexual fluids to the potion.

Step 4. Place an item representing yourself progressively closer and closer to the Passive Substitution. After you have allowed the spell to run over the course of an odd number of days, tie the two items together.

Step 5. Red for love; pink for romance. Use one of these or both together for a romantic love affair. To add the element of purity, include a white candle on your altar arrangement. Your candles, altar cloth and the string or ribbon you use to bind your prospective lover to you should all reflect these color associations. At the end of this spell, you might enfold the items involved into a piece of used, unlaundered red or pink bedsheet to symbolize the person coming to your bed.

Step 6. Charge the spell using your own accumulated life force; use incantation or ask a spirit associated with love to help you charge the items in this spell.

Step 7. Bury the refuse from this spell in your backyard or keep it in a bag behind or underneath your bed until your desire is fulfilled.

Lesson 2.
Prosperity Spell

Step 1. Thursday (or planetary hour of Jupiter) during a Waxing or Full Moon; Moon in Aries or Taurus.

Step 2. Since this spell is to be cast on the abstract idea of prosperity rather than directly on a business or employment situation, you may select a green candle, particularly a green cat-shaped candle to represent prosperity coming into your home.

Step 3. Choose Money Drawing, Prosperity or a similar potion

Step 4. Apply the potion to the candle using a motion toward you to mimic the flow of prosperity

Step 5. Green for money and prosperity; gold for riches and wealth.

Step 6. Charge the candle by meditation. Write an incantation, for example, "Money, money come to me, in abundance three times." Optionally, ask for assistance from a spirit you work with.

Step 7. Release the energy of this spell into a High John the Conqueror root; citrine, aventurine or other talisman related to prosperity. Carry this item with you.

Lesson 3.
Spell to Increase Physical Strength and Determination

Step 1. Tuesday (or planetary hour of Mars); Waxing Moon; Moon in Aries for vigor or Moon in Taurus for tenacity

Step 2. Examples of objects that represent strength are a bull figurine, a red candle in the shape of a devil, an image of the Hindu god Shiva or any object that represents strength and determination to you personally

Step 3. Power Drawing or a similar potion.

Step 4. Optionally, do something to the Passive Substitution that represents strength to you. For example, place the object in the direct sunlight at sunrise on Tuesday, which is the day ruled by the planet Mars.

Step 5. Red.

Step 6. Charge the object; use incantation or call upon the power of a spirit such as Shiva, Mars or Thor to empower your spell.

Step 7. Release the power of this spell directly upon yourself by applying the potion to your clothing. Alternatively, place the potion in a mojo bag and carry its influence with you.

Lesson 4.
Spell to Ace a Test

Step 1. Wednesday (or planetary hour of Mercury); Waxing Moon; Moon in Gemini.

Step 2. An item that represents the test, which may be a manual or simply the name of the test, the name of the class, the date the test is to be taken and any other details that identify it written on a piece of plain paper.

Step 3. Success in All Endeavors or similar potion.

Step 4. Place something that represents yourself, such as a Personal Effect or photo, on top of the test to show your dominance over it. Alternatively, turn the paper with the name of the test on it 90 degrees and write your name over it nine times, completely crossing and covering it with your signature to show your dominance.

Step 5. Yellow for education and orange for career.

Step 6. Charge the potion; optionally, write an incantation or ask for the assistance of a spirit such as Thoth, Mercury or Hermes for wisdom or Mars for success.

Step 7. Apply the charged potion to yourself, the objects that represent the test or other success talisman and keep it with you to impart its influence.

Lesson 5.
Spell to Win at Poker

Step 1. Tuesday (or planetary hour of Mars); Waxing or Full Moon; Moon in Aries.

Step 2. As a Passive Substitution for poker, choose a new poker deck. You may arrange the following cards in a Royal Flush in the suit of diamonds, which represent wealth: Ace, King, Queen, Jack and Ten. Alternatively, write representations of these cards on a plain piece of paper, use a High John the Conqueror root (the gambler's charm) or choose any other item that represents a winning poker hand to you.

Step 3. Apply Three Jacks and a King, High John the Conqueror, Black Cat or any other suitable potion to the cards. Optionally, include a drop of your own blood to add power and dominance. If you are using a different object, apply the oil to it.

Step 4. Inscribe your name and a phrase that states your desire to win at poker onto the side of the candle you use for this spell. Apply potion to the Passive Substitution and place something that represents you on top of it or cross and cover it by turning it 90 degrees and writing your name nine times over the top of it.

Step 5. Green, gold, yellow or blue.

Step 6. Charge the items; optionally, write an incantation or call upon a spirit like San Maximon to assist you.

Step 7. Release the energy of this spell upon the Passive Substitution and carry it with you. If it is five winning cards or a paper, place them in the bottom of your right shoe for dominance in this matter. If you are using a charm like a High John the Conqueror root, anoint it with the gambling or luck potion and place it in your pocket where you can touch it while you play cards.

Lesson 6.
Spell to Stop Neighbors from Gossiping

Step 1. Saturday (or planetary hour of Saturn); Waxing Moon; Moon in Capricorn.

Step 2. Classically, a beef tongue is used to represent the gossips, together with their Personal Effects or papers with their names written on them. Slice the tongue open and insert the papers or Personal Effects.

Step 3. Stop Gossip (Tapa la Boca) or a similar potion; slippery elm is a classic "shut up" herb. Speed the action of this spell by adding a little dragon's blood or cinnamon to the potion.

Step 4. Baptize the beef tongue in the name of your enemies, then act upon it by means of nine needles or nails to sew it up or immobilize it. Then, you may put it in the freezer to "freeze" the tongues of the gossips.

Step 5. Black

Step 6. Charge the objects in the spell; optionally, write an incantation or employ the assistance of a spirit like San Ramón Nonato, who is known for his power to stop gossip.

Step 7. Bury the items from this spell at the nearest crossroad and return home without looking over your shoulder. Alternatively, some practitioners remove all of the Personal Effects and sharp objects from the tongue, cook it and eat it.

Lesson 7.
Spell to Gain the Admiration and Approval of Others

Step 1. Friday (or planetary hour of Venus) for affection and social situations or Sunday (or planetary hour of the Sun) for approval and fame; Full Moon; Moon in Leo.

Step 2. Use a photograph of yourself or your Personal Effects placed inside an effigy of wax or cloth to represent yourself.

Step 3. Admiration Oil or similar potion made of herbs or stones that have properties associated with the Sun.

Step 4. Place a representation of your popularity on the Passive Substitution. This may be a drawing or an actual object such as an award, a crown, a laurel wreath or any other object that represents the approval of others to you.

Step 5. Pink for affection and gold for fame

Step 6. Charge the objects; write an incantation or ask for the assistance of a spirit associated with the Sun, such as Apollo or the spirit of a greatly admired person who has passed on.

Step 7. Release the energy of this spell upon yourself by placing the refuse of this spell into a charm, which you charge upon the altar along with the other spell items. Carry the amulet with you. Then, bury the refuse of this spell in a favorite place in your front yard or near your door step. Alternatively, place it in a drawer or closet where it will not be found or touched by anyone, so that it imparts its influence to you inside your home.

Lesson 8.
Spell to Break an Emotional Attachment

Step 1. Saturday (or planetary hour of Saturn); Waning Moon; Moon in Aquarius or Moon in Taurus.

Step 2. Choose figure candles to represent yourself and your ex-friend. Attach Personal Effects from each of you. Alternatively, use two cords or ribbons to represent each of you. There are numerous other possibilities for representing each party involved in the situation.

Step 3. Make a potion of herbs such as amaranth, bittersweet, witch hazel and rue.

Step 4. Tie a cord around the two Passive Substitutions that represent you and your ex-friend, then cut them to symbolize that your emotional tie is severed. Use scissors or a knife to cut the power of this emotional tie. You may use nine cords and cut them over a period of nine nights as you conduct the spell. Alternatively, tie nine knots in two cords that represent you and your ex-friend to symbolized your emotional connection, then untie them one by one to represent the loosing of this emotional bond.

Step 5. Black for severing the tie; red or pink to symbolize the feelings of love or friendship.

Step 6. Charge the objects in this spell; recite an incantation revolving around your emotions and your severing of these emotions to chant as you perform your Imitative Action.

Step 7. Burn the refuse from this spell and cast the ashes into running water. Alternatively, bury it at the roots of a tree in a cemetery.

Lesson 9.
Protection Spell for Your Car

Step 1. Monday (or planetary hour of the Moon) for protection, Wednesday (or planetary hour of Mercury) for travel; Full Moon; Moon in Gemini or Moon in Sagittarius.

Step 2. A photograph of your car or the car, itself.

Step 3. St. Christopher Oil, Safe Travel, Protection from Thieves or other relevant potion or herbs.

Step 4. Symbolize the protection of your vehicle by sprinkling blessed Sea Salt around the Passive Substitution upon your altar. Alternatively, sprinkle it with a protective potion and place a protective talisman on top of it. If you're working with St. Christopher, place a prayer card, statue or medal on top of it to show that your car is under his protection.

Step 5. White

Step 6. Charge the objects; write an incantation or ask for the assistance of a spirit associated with protection and travel, such as St. Christopher, Michael the Archangel, Santa Muerte, an ancestral spirit or any spirit you work with who can help you.

Step 7. Release the energy directly upon the object of the spell by anointing your car with the charged potions and by placing the items from this working inside your vehicle.

Lesson 10.
Spell to Get Someone to Sign a Divorce Agreement

Step 1. Sunday (or planetary hour of the Sun) for court cases and family concerns; Waning Moon; Moon in Libra

Step 2. The contract or a copy of it

Step 3. Domination or High John the Conquer combined with your own blood or powdered nail clippings for increased domination power

Step 4. Skull image or an actual animal skull. If you use a white skull candle, carve out the bottom and add your own personal effects. The skull represents your mental domination of this matter, so you will place it on top of the anointed contract.

Step 5. Brown candle for contracts, court and legal matters. Alternatively, green is used for legal matters when working with Latin American spirits; use white or bone-colored candles and other objects for protection and peace in the home. Use one or a combination of these colors at your discretion.

Step 6. Charge the items involved in the spell; recite an incantation or one of numerous prayers or Psalms for protection and invite a protective spirits such as Santa Muerte, Saint Michael or an ancestor who has passed on to assist you.

Step 7. Release the spell directly upon the contract or its copy by anointing the edges with the oil or sprinkling with the powder or passing it through the incense smoke of the potion.

APPENDIX

Common Potions

The following are a few common formulas for magical oils, powders, incense, baths, washes and other potions, which may be purchased from many metaphysical bookstores, botanicas and online shops. They may, also, be made using the *Traditional Witches' Formulary and Potion-making Guide: Recipes for Magical Oils, Powders and Other Potions* by this author.

Admiration: To garner the respect and admiration of others

Banishing: To banish an enemy

Black Cat: Good luck; bad luck reversal and good luck gambling

Court Case: For success in court

Domination: To dominate in any matter; used in games, business and inter-personal relationships

Fiery Wall of Protection: For powerful protection from enemies and dark forces

Goofer Dust: For protection and exorcism when carried. When deployed against an enemy it is used to cause illness, confusion and sometimes death

High John the Conqueror: Domination and success at gambling

Home Protection: To bless and protect your domicile

Hot Foot Powder: To drive away enemies

Law Keep Away (Contra la Ley): For protection from law enforcement agents of any kind

Love and Lust: To inspire love and lust in another person

Love Attraction: To draw love

Money Drawing: To attract money

Power Drawing: For strength and physical power

Prosperity: To draw abundance and wealth

Protection from Thieves: To guard against theft

Quitting Powder: To stop harassment and get people to leave you alone

Safe Travel: For safety when traveling by any means

Saint Christopher: For protection during travel and to protect your car

Separation: To break up friends or a couple

Stop Gossip (Tapa la Boca): To make people stop talking about you

Success in All Endeavors: To accomplish whatever you desire

Super Fast Luck: For immediate good luck

Three Jacks and a King: To win at card games

Common Roots and Herbs

The following are a few common roots and herbs that may be applied to your spells:

Amaranth: Protection from the evil eye and to heal a broken heart

Basil: Love and to keep a lover faithful; protection; exorcism; wealth and success in business

Bittersweet: Protection; healing and to heal a broken heart

Blessed Thistle: Home protection; exorcism and healing

Calendula (Pot Marigold): To win in court; luck in the lottery and prophetic dreams

Caraway: Protection from thieves

Cinnamon: Love; speedy action

Dandelion: Fulfill secret longings; to break hexes; to call spirits; psychic dreams and divination

Dragon's Blood: Protection; power

Eucalyptus: Healing and death

Garlic: Protection from evil spirits and evil people

Ginseng root: Love; energy; youth; vigor; health; prosperity

High John the Conqueror root: Dominance, command; control; success in all endeavors; a primary gambling charm

Jezebel root: Domination

Lavender: Peace; happiness; purification; tranquility and pleasant dreams

Marigold: Protection; legal matters; psychic abilities; visions and dreams

Orris root: Feminine power

Plumeria: Admiration

Rosemary: Love; health; peace in the home; to gain power over a man

Rue: Good luck, protection; prosperity and regrets

Sandalwood: Enhanced psychic abilities; spirit communication

Slippery Elm: To stop gossip

Thyme: Used in love spells and divination; sleep; purification; courage; money and psychic abilities

Witch Hazel: Protection and to heal a broken heart

Wormwood: Love; protection; to call spirits and to cause trouble and strife for enemies

Yarrow: Divination regarding love; understanding of animals; courage and exorcism

Trees

Alder: Divination and prophesy

Almond: Power; strength and clairvoyance

Apple: Immortality; youth and love

Ash: Sacrifice and spirit communication

Beech: Peace

Birch: Divination; purification; rejuvenation and renewal

Bonsai: Peace; balance and good fortune

Cedar: Protection and exorcism

Cherry: Prophesy

Cypress: Death and the underworld

Dogwood: Power and beauty

Elder: Healing and protection

Elm: Strong will

Fir: Rebirth and immortality

Hawthorn: Fertility; fidelity; happiness and good luck fishing

Hazel: Divination and wisdom

Holly: Protection; death and rebirth

Malabar Chestnut: Money and wealth: known as the "money tree."

Maple: Hope

Oak: Strength; power; courage; fidelity and protection

Olive: Peace and harmony

Palm: Prosperity; success and fertility

Pine: Creativity; healing; longevity and immortality

Rowan: Protection and exorcism

Walnut: Protection and healing

Willow: Divination; healing; mourning and death

Yew: Death; rebirth; strength; healing; prophesy and divination

Zoological Effects and Other Objects

The following is a list of correspondences for zoological effects and related images, which may be used as Passive Substitutions, usually to represent abstract ideas or as Active Substitutions to cause a particular effect upon a target.

Animals, Reptiles, Insects and Fantastic Beings

Ant: An army; industry

Ass (Jack Ass): Sacred to the Egyptian god Typhon; a beast of burden; a means of conveyance

Bat: Spirits and death; a trickster spirit

Beaver: Home; industry

Bees: Industry; the queen bee represents authority and privilege; feminine power; matriarchal society; bee goddesses (Artemis); business; social networking; a medium for sending and receiving messages from the spirit world

Birds: Creatures of god; spirits of the air; messengers of the gods; a bird carrying a snake is a symbol of Lucifer

Buffalo: Ancestral spirits; the satisfaction of physical and spiritual needs

Bull: The Bull Cult; the Apis Bull Cult of Egypt; the Bull of Memphis; a symbol of the Age of Taurus; the pre-Christian era; great power, physical strength and determination. A creature of the earth; sacred to Shiva and a symbol of male fertility

Butterfly: Metamorphosis; the psyche; the spirit.

Buzzard: A scavenger; cruelty

Camel: Transportation; survival

Cat: The goddess Diana; Bast; guardian of the house; good and bad luck; healing emanations; the consort of witches

Corvid: A bad omen; a bird of death

Cow: Wealth; sustenance

Coyote: A leader; transformation; skill; the road opener

Deer: The soul

Dog: Loyalty; protection; Sirius the Dog Star; sacred to Mercury

Dolphin: Sacred to Apollo and Neptune

Donkey: (See Ass)

Dove: The Holy Ghost; the spirit; wisdom; sacred to Astarte, Cybele, Isis, Venus, Juno, Aphrodite and Mary

Dragon: The lineage of kings; guardian of treasure

Duck: Migration; travel

Eagle: Ascendancy; domination from above; swift movement; justice; keen sight; vision

Elephant: Good luck; Lord Ganesha

Falcon: A bird of prey

Firefly: Illumination; a flash of insight

Fish: Sacred to the Greeks: A symbol of the Age of Pisces; associated with Aphrodite; beauty; mysticism; happiness and good fortune

Fly: A tormentor; an irritation; Lord of the Flies; the Chaldean god Baal; Beelzebub, Lord of the Flies ("My Lord who hums"); bedevilment

Fox: Trickery; cunning; malice

Frog or Toad: Fertility; a creature of air and water; transformation; adaptability; rain; rebirth; a creature of transitions; of both water and earth; secret identity

Goat: A sacrifice, a scapegoat

Goose: Knowledge; silliness; gossip

Hare: (See rabbit)

Hawk: Perception; keenness of vision; a broad view of a matter

Hen: Abundance; life; supernatural forces; guardian of treasure; guardian of power; the black hen is a symbol of the devil

Hippo: Protects from grave robbers; associated with Typhon and Mars

Hog (Sow): Good luck; associated with Diana

Hornet: A dangerous situation

Horse: Protection; to protect cattle and other creatures; to guard wealth; to ward off evil spirits; the horse's head was used in Scandinavia as an instrument of malefic witchcraft to place curses

Hummingbird: Romantic love

Jackal: A predator

Lion: Strength; courage; supremacy; glory; vigilance, divine guardianship (placed at entryways); domination

Lizard: Regeneration; survival

Locust: A plague; a disturbance; destruction; passion; disease; hate; strife; an act of god

Magpie: A mimic; a thief; exceedingly sly

Mosquito: Irritation; disease

Nightingale: A muse; artistic inspiration

Octopus: Control; multiple interests

Ostrich: A bird that cannot fly; a symbol of denial

Owl: Wisdom; the watcher; to see what is hidden; eyes in the night; associated with Hecate; Semiramis; Ishtar and Lilith; a common form for a witch's familiar

Oyster: Hidden treasure; a pearl

Peacock: Pride; Beauty; a symbol of Lucifer and Malek Taus, the Blue Angel

Pelican: Self-sacrifice

Phoenix: Renewal; rebirth; recovery from disaster

Pig: (See Hog)

Python (Snake): A constrictor; a constricting or suffocating situation

Rabbit: Cunning; intelligence; swiftness; sexuality

Raven (Corvid): "The devil's bird," a thief; an omen of death

Rooster: An announcement; male (sexual) aggression; associated with Aries, the rising sun and East.

Salamander: Transition; survival; adaptability; disguise; camouflage; the element of fire

Scarab: The soul; resurrection; renewal; strength of the body; virility; strength; courage; the god of the sun; associated with Ra

Scorpion: The betrayer; male sexuality; death; the occult; regeneration; wisdom; self-destruction; a backbiter; false and deceitful

Skunk: Justice

Snail: Slow but steady progress; self-sufficiency

Snake (Serpent): Wisdom; the earth; cleverness; Lord of the Earth; vengeance; death; poison; king of reptiles. Used to cause mental suffering, insanity and headaches

Spider: A cunning individual; one who lays plans, contrives, traps and binds

Squirrel: Destruction; elusiveness; chatter, gossip, psychological cruelty

Swan: Transitions; enchantment; beauty

Tiger: Aggression; maternal power

Toad: (See Frog)

Turkey: Food; clothing; work; worldly needs are met

Turtle: Fertility; patience

Unicorn: The spirit; a pure spirit; a symbol of the Christ; healing; godliness

Vulture: Greed; aggression

Whale: Generosity

Wolf: Treachery; male sexual predator; selfishness; greediness; self-interest; debauchery; craftiness

Worm: Regeneration; interference

Natural Objects

Use these objects when you find them in nature. Never harm an animal or endanger yourself to acquire them.

Bark of a Lightning Struck Tree: To cause destruction; to destroy and enemy

Black Dog Hairs: Dark arts; cursing and hexing

Black Hen Feathers: Cursing and hexing

Bones: Death; to cause death and to have power over it

Cat's Claws: To acquire something you desire

Cat's Whiskers: Invisibility

Hives: Masonry; mind control; Venus and women

Locust Shells: To cause plagues and destruction

Shells: Magnetic feminine energy. Powdered seashells are used to hex and curse. Cowrie shells are used in divination.

Silk: Silk cloth is used to wrap charged objects to maintain their energy. Silk maintains and conducts metaphysical energy.

Spider Webs: To bind; to trap

Wasp and Hornet Nests: To torment an enemy and cause insanity

Other Objects

These are common household, agricultural and other mundane objects which can be applied to spells and potions.

Coins: Money and wealth

Cone: Power vortex

Horseshoes: Protection and good luck.

Knives or Swords: Defense and destruction

Lamp: Illumination; revelations; knowledge

Nails: Iron nails, coffin nails; protection; dark arts

Needles: Protection from evil people and the Evil Eye. To ward off evil, especially when the eye of the needle is broken. Used to direct energy to a target and to cause pain and death.

Pins: Used to direct energy at a target

Salt: To ward of evil and to destroy enemies.

Scissors or Shears: To cut the power of someone or something

Sieve: Representative of clouds because it causes drops of water to fall. Used to cause rain and storms.

Two Dollar Bills: Good fortune

Common Gemstones

Amethyst: Calming

Aventurine: Financial matters

Black Obsidian: Creativity; protection and to dispel negativity

Bloodstone: Invisibility; courage; generosity and healing

Citrine: Money and prosperity; called "the merchant's stone"

Clear Quartz: Amplifies energy; neutral

Dalmation Jasper: Balance; harmony; opportunity and to destroy obstacles

Emerald: Wealth and clarity

Garnet: Passion and power

Jade: Good luck; protection; prosperity and wealth

Jet: Protection from evil; purification

Lapis Lazuli: Psychic abilities; communication and healing

Malachite: Protection from psychic attack

Meteorites and Tektites: Relationship with the gods, extra-terrestrials and transformation

Moonstone: Intuition and insight

Moss Agate: Health; fast healing and wealth

Onyx: Protection

Rhodonite: Love; tranquility; friendship

Rose Quartz: To attract love and to heal the heart

Ruby: Passion; protection from psychic attack

Tiger's Eye: Enhance psychic abilities; clairvoyance

Turquoise: Good luck moving or traveling; good fortune; prosperity

Planetary Correspondences to Gemstone Minerals

The following planetary and zodiac correspondences are derived from the text of Manly P. Hall's, *The Secret Teachings of All Ages*, first published in 1928. He compiled them from the writings of "Paracelsus, Agrippa, Kircher, Lilly, and numerous other magicians and astrologers."

Sun: Carbuncle, ruby, garnet – especially the pyrope – and other fiery stones, sometimes the diamond; to the moon, the pearl, selenite, and other forms of crystal

Saturn: Onyx, jasper, topaz, and sometimes the lapis lazuli

Jupiter: Sapphire, emerald, and marble

Mars: Amethyst, hyacinth, lodestone, sometimes the diamond

Venus: Turquoise, beryl, emerald, and sometimes the pearl, alabaster, coral, and carnelian

Mercury: Chrysolite, agate, and variegated marble.

Zodiac Correspondences to Gemstone Minerals

Aries: Sardonyx, bloodstone, amethyst, and diamond

Taurus: Carnelian, turquoise, hyacinth, sapphire, moss agate, and emerald

Gemini: Topaz, agate, chrysoprase, crystal, and aquamarine

Cancer: Topaz, chalcedony, black onyx, moonstone, pearl, cat's-eye, crystal, and sometimes the emerald

Leo: Jasper, sardonyx, beryl, ruby, chrysolite, amber, tourmaline, sometimes the diamond

Virgo: Emerald, carnelian, jade, chrysolite, and sometimes the pink jasper and hyacinth

Libra: Beryl, sardius, coral, lapis lazuli, opal, and sometimes the diamond

Scorpio: Amethyst, beryl, sardonyx, aquamarine, carbuncle, lodestone, topaz, and malachite

Sagittarius: Hyacinth, topaz, chrysolite, emerald, carbuncle, and turquoise

Capricorn: Chrysoprase, ruby, malachite, black onyx, white onyx, jet, and moonstone

Aquarius: Clear quartz crystal, sapphire, garnet, zircon, and opal

Pisces: Sapphire, jasper, chrysolite, moonstone, and amethyst

Planetary Correspondences to Metals

Lead: Saturn

Copper: Venus

Quicksilver (Mercury): Mercury

Gold: Sun

Silver: Moon

Antimony: Earth

Uranium: Uranus

Radium: Neptune

Spirits

The following is a list of spirits from around the world upon whom you may call for assistance in your spell work according to their specialization:

Apollo: Masculine beauty; youth and health

Diana: Love; beauty and a successful hunt

Eleggua: Crossroads; success and destroyer of obstacles

Frigga: Love; marriage and maternity

Hecate: Underworld; death; healing; rejuvenation; rebirth; witchcraft; occult knowledge and power

Hermes, Mercury or Thoth: Wisdom; communication; the arts and successful selling

Jove or Jupiter: Abundance and expansion

Lord Ganesha: Success; money and destroyer of obstacles

Lucifer: Knowledge and illumination

Mars: War; vigorous action; speed; success

Saint Michael the Archangel: Exorcism and vigorous protection from evil

San Cipriano: Occult knowledge; patron saint of magicians

San Maximon (Maam): Gambling; good luck; money and love

Santa Muerte: Protection; revenge; spirit communication; death; rejuvenation; second chances; love and unlimited other powers

Shiva: Power; destruction; strength; vigor; masculine energy

Thor: Strength and protection

Typhon: Destruction

Venus: Love and beauty

GLOSSARY

Active Substitution: A representation of the influence you want to create on an object or its Passive Substitution. It is often a potion or some other substance.

Air: A medium that provides an equilibrium between Fire and Water.

Akasha: The fifth element, which is the precursor to the other four elements of fire, water, air and earth. An element of dynamic spirit; the quintessence.

Allopathy: Conventional Western medicine.

Altar: Work space. A place set aside for magical workings.

Amulet: A charm or talisman.

Anoint: To apply oil to a person or object.

Botanica: A metaphysical store that specializes in products common to Spanish-speaking countries.

Censer: Thurible or incense burner.

Charge: The act of infusing an object with elemental energy.

Charms: Objects intended to bring good fortune and protect from evil.

Conjure: To call upon; to invoke or manifest.

Consecrate: To set aside an item for a particular purpose. The act of consecration generally involves saying a prayer, essentially speaking to the energy of the item to enhance its power and bring it under your will.

Contagious Magic: The transference of energy from one object to another.

Crossed: The condition of having an accumulation of negative energy.

Curse: A malefic spell intended to do grave harm.

Divination: A method of obtaining information about the past, present or future.

Doctrine of Signatures: The principle that the metaphysical and healing properties of plants and minerals can sometimes be ascertained on the basis of their physical qualities, such as color, shape of the leaves, fruits, blossoms, scent and other characteristics.

Dowsing: The use of a divining rod, pendulum or similar device to find lost articles, minerals and water and to acquire a broad range of other information.

Dress: To anoint an object; to apply oil to a candle, talisman or other object.

Dynamic Ether: The field through which energetic signals pass.

Earth: This element is formed by the union of fire, water and air. It is the most densely physical of the four basic elements. It is the principle most closely related to physical existence.

Elemental: An entity; force or spirit of the four elements; earth, water, air or fire. According to the alchemist, Paracelsus, the four basic varieties of spirits are gnomes, undines or nymphs, sylphs, and salamanders.

Ether: The fifth element, akasha or the akashic field.

Etheric Body: The energetic field of the human body that is causal to the physical body. In second wave Theosophy, the etheric body is the field nearest the physical body, itself.

Evocation: Conjuration or summoning of a spirit, usually by means of incantation.

Familiar: A spiritual being of an elemental nature; sometimes a demonic spirit; sometimes a thought form created to act as a servant. Also, called a servitor or a familiar spirit.

Feed: To energize and maintain the energy of a magical object or familiar spirit to keep it alive.

Fire: Heat and expansion. It is the active element of the electrical force.

Five Elements: Akasha or ether, fire, water, air and earth. Akasha gave birth to the other four elements, the first being fire.

Four Elements: Fire, water, air and earth.

Glory Be Prayer: "Glory be to the Father and to the Son and to the Holy Spirit, as it was in the beginning, is now and ever shall be, world without end. Amen."

Grimoire: A spell book. This term was applied to occult books of the Middle Ages. A modern form of the grimoire is the Book of Shadows; this term is borrowed from Wicca and refers to a spell book or manual of procedures belonging to an individual or a coven.

Hail Mary Prayer: "Hail Mary, full of grace. Our Lord is with thee. Blessed art thou among women and blessed is the fruit of thy womb, Jesus. Holy Mary, Mother of God, pray for us sinners, now and at the hour of our death. Amen."

Hex: A spell, especially one intended to cause misfortune.

Homeopathic Magic: Sympathetic magic.

Homeopathy: A healing system that involves the manipulation of substances of energy similar to the organ or disease to be treated.

Hoodoo: A general term for American witchcraft practices originating in Africa and blended with Native American practices, Kabbalism and European folk magic.

Imitative Action: A physical act performed on the object of a spell or its Passive Substitution that mimics the influence you want to bring to bear on the person or thing itself.

Incantation: A chant or a mantra. Powerful words recited over an object to direct its energy.

Invocation: Conjuration or summoning of a spirit, usually by means of incantation. To make a personal connection with the spirit, sometimes taking on its powers and abilities.

Kabbalah (Kabala or Qabbālâ): A Hebrew system of thought. A prominent feature of the Kabbalah is the "Tree of Life," which provides a complex map and a key to the construction of the universe and everything in it.

Magic: The art and science of effecting change in the physical world by metaphysical means.

Mojo Bag: An approximately 2" by 3" flannel or cotton bag with a drawstring. A talisman or "hand" assembled to create a particular effect and regularly charged or fed.

Novena: A series of Catholic-style prayers conducted over the course of nine consecutive days.

Our Father Prayer: "Our Father which art in heaven, Hallowed be thy name. Thy kingdom come, Thy will be done in earth, as it is in heaven. Give us this day our daily bread. And forgive us our debts, as we forgive our debtors. And lead us not into temptation, but deliver us from evil: For thine is the kingdom, and the power, and the glory, for ever. Amen."

Parapsychology: The scientific study of psychic abilities and other aspects of the paranormal.

Passive Substitution: The object to be acted upon or its representation, which has the same or a similar vibratory harmonic as the person or object you want to influence.

Personal Effects: Items that carry a person's unique, vibrational harmonic frequency. For example, blood, other bodily fluids, hair, underwear, signature or a photograph; also, called personal concerns.

Petition: A specific request made to a spirit, which is usually written down.

Poppet: An effigy or a doll. A representation of a person made of wax, cloth or other material.

Prayer: A request made to a spirit; an invocation or evocation; sometimes a set recitation, such as the Our Father or the Glory Be.

Psalms: A book of the Old Testament, which is a powerful grimoire commonly used in American Hoodoo and Mexican Witchcraft.

Subtle Field: An energetic field, composed of sub-fields, which are causal to the things in physical existence.

Sympathetic Magic: The esoteric science of correspondences or similarities between objects that makes use of things with a similar vibration to create an influence.

Talisman: An amulet. An object that has magical powers.

Tetragrammaton: The four elements expressed Kabbalistically as "Yod He Vau He" and sometimes abbreviated as "JHVH." This concept was later anthropomorphized as "God" and his name is pronounced "Jehovah" or "Ya-weh" by Jews and Christians.

Thurible: Censer. An incense burner.

Transference, Principle of: A principle that involves the movement of metaphysical energy and properties from one object to another. Sometimes called "contagious magic."

Uncrossing: A spell or ritual intended to reverse a crossed condition.

Voodoo: African-based spiritual and religious practices commonly found in New Orleans, Memphis and, historically, elsewhere in the mid-west and the south of the U.S. This American spelling is used to differentiate it from Haitian Vodou.

Water: The opposite of fire, its properties are coolness and contraction. It is the receptive element of the electrical force.

Wicca: A religion based on a form of initiatory witchcraft founded by Gerald Gardner in the 1950s. It is of two basic types: British Traditional Wicca and Neo-wicca.

Witchcraft: A worldwide practice, which is based on esoteric scientific principles.

Work Space: An altar; a place where rituals or spells are conducted.

Working: A spell or ritual; also, called a "job" or "laying down a trick" in Hoodoo.

Zoological Effects: Objects obtained from an animal or insect; sometimes representations of these things; also, called zoological concerns.

REFERENCES

1. Redgrove, Herbert Stanley, *Being a Series of Excursions in the Byways of Thought*, 1920 http://www.sacred-texts.com/etc/bb/index.htm

2. Sir James George Frazer, *The Golden Bough*, 1922, P. 2. http://www.bartleby.com/196/6.html

3. Ibid.

4. Dyer, T.F. Thiselton, *Folk-lore of Shakespeare*, 1883, P. 34. http://www.sacred-texts.com/sks/flos/flos04.htm

5. Lawrence, Robert Means, *The Magic of the Horse-Shoe With Other Folk-Lore Notes*, 1898. http://www.sacred-texts.com/etc/mhs/

6. Ibid.

7. Ibid.

8. Constable, Trevor James, "The Work of Dr. Ruth Drown: An Outline on a Thumbnail" *Journal of Borderland Research* (Vol. XVII, No. 1, January – February 1961. http://journal.borderlands.com/2010/radionics-ruth-drown-and-qaballah/

9. Besant, Annie, C.W. Leadbeater and Curuppumullage Jinarajadasa, *Occult Chemistry: Investigations by Clairvoyant Magnification into the Structure of the Atoms of the Periodic Table and Some Compounds*, 1908. http://www.gutenberg.org/files/16058/16058-h/16058-h.htm

10. *Blavatsky Study Center,* Lucifer, "H.P. Blavatsky's London Magazine," http://www.blavatskyarchives.com/luciferreprints.htm

11. Buriss, Eli Edward, *Taboo, Magic, Spirits: A Study of Primitive Elements in Roman Religion*, 1931. http://www.sacred-texts.com/cla/tms/tms08.htm

BIBLIOGRAPHY

Resources for Information About the Powers of Herbs, Minerals and Potions

Bardon, Franz, *Initiation into Hermetics*, Merkur Publishing, 2009

Bardon, Franz, *The Practice of Magical Evocation*, Merkur Pub, 2nd edition, 2001.

Bardon, Franz, *The Key to the True Quabbalah: The Quabbalist as a Sovereign in the Microcosm and the Microcosm*, Dieter Ruggerbert, Wuppertal, Germany, 1956.

Besant, Annie, C.W. Leadbeater and Curuppumullage Jinarajadasa, *Occult Chemistry: Investigations by Clairvoyant Magnification into the Structure of the Atoms of the Periodic Table and Some Compounds*, 1908. http://www.gutenberg.org/files/16058/16058-h/16058-h.htm

Beyerl, Paul, *The Master Book of Herbalism*, Phoenix Publishing, 1984.

Cosimano, Chuck, *Psionic Power*, Llewellyn, 1989.

Culpeper, Nicholas, *Complete Herbal*, 1643. http://archive.org/details/cu31924001353279)

Cunningham, Scott, *Cunningham's Encyclopedia of Crystal, Gem & Metal Magic* (Cunningham's Encyclopedia Series), Llewellyn Publications, 1998.

Cunningham, Scott, Cunningham's Encyclopedia of Magical Herbs (Cunningham's Encyclopedia Series), Llewellyn Publications, 1985.

DiGregorio, Sophia, *Traditional Witches' Formulary and Potion-making Guide: Recipes for Magical Oils, Powders and Other Potions*, Winter Tempest Books, 2012.

Hall, Judy, *Crystal Bible*, Walking Stick Press, 2003.

Huson, Paul, *Mastering Herbalism: A Practical Guide,* Madison Books, 2001.

Kraig, Donald Michael, *Modern Magick: Eleven Lessons in the High Magickal Arts*, Llewellyn Publications, 1988.

Mathers, S.L. MacGregor, translator, *The Kabbalah Unveiled,* 1912. http://www.sacred-texts.com/jud/tku/index.htm

Melody and Julianne Guilbault, *Love is in the Earth: A Kaleidoscope of Crystals: The Reference Book Describing the Metaphysical Properties of the Mineral Kingdom*, Earth Love Pub House, 3rd edition, 1995.

Mullins, Eustance, *Murder by Injection*, National Council for Medical Research; 1995.

Powell, A.E., *The Etheric Double,* 1925.

Regardie, Israel, *A Garden Of Pomegranates: A Outline of the Qabalah*, Llewellyn Publishing, 3rd edition, 1974.

Tansley, David, *Rays and Radionics*, C.W. Daniel & Co., 1984.

Thorsson, Edred, *Futhark: A Handbook of Rune Magic*, Weiser, 2012.

MORE WINTER TEMPEST BOOKS

If you enjoyed this book, you might enjoy other Winter Tempest Books:

All Natural Dental Remedies: Herbs and Home Remedies to Heal Your Teeth & Naturally Restore Tooth Enamel by Angela Kaelin

Black Magic for Dark Times: Spells of Revenge and Protection by Angela Kaelin

Blood and Black Roses: A Dark Bouquet of Vampires, Romance and Horror by Sophia diGregorio (Fiction)

The Forgotten: The Vampire Prince by Sophia diGregorio (Fiction)

Grimoire of Santa Muerte: Spells and Rituals of Most Holy Death, the Unofficial Saint of Mexico by Sophia diGregorio

How to Communicate with Spirits: Séances, Ouija Boards and Summoning by Angela Kaelin

How to Develop Advanced Psychic Abilities: Obtain Information about the Past, Present and Future Through Clairvoyance by Sophia diGregorio

How to Read the Tarot for Fun, Profit and Psychic Development for Beginners and Advanced Readers by Angela Kaelin

Magical Healing: How to Use Your Mind to Heal Yourself and Others by Angela Kaelin

Natural Remedies for Reversing Gray Hair: Nutrition and Herbs for Anti-aging and Optimum Health by Thomas W. Xander

Practical Black Magic: How to Hex and Curse Your Enemies by Sophia diGregorio

Spells for Money and Wealth by Angela Kaelin

To Conjure the Perfect Man by Sophia diGregorio (Fiction)

The Traditional Witches' Book of Love Spells by Angela Kaelin

Traditional Witches' Formulary and Potion-making Guide: Recipes for Magical Oils, Powders and Other Potions by Sophia diGregorio

ABOUT THE AUTHOR

Sophia diGregorio is a long-time student and practitioner of the occult, a professional psychic and a fan of Gothic horror. Her fiction weaves together paranormal themes and Gothic fantasy with characters and situations drawn from real life. Her non-fiction titles are based on her own 20-some years of experience and research into the world of the occult.

Disclaimer: The author and publisher of this guide has used her best efforts in preparing this document. The author makes no representation or warranties with respect to the accuracy, applicability, fitness or completeness of the contents of this document. The author disclaims any warranties expressed or implied. The author of this book is not a medical or legal professional and is not qualified to give medical or legal advice. Nothing in this document should be construed as medical or legal advice. The material in this book is presented for informational purposes only. Nothing in this book should be construed as incitement to dangerous or illegal acts and the reader is advised to be aware of and heed all pertinent laws in his or her city, state, country or other jurisdiction. Any medical or legal questions should be addressed to the proper medical or legal authorities. The author shall in no event be held liable for any losses or damages, including but not limited to special, incidental, consequential or other damages incurred by the use of this information. The statements in this book have not been evaluated by any government organization. The statements contained herein represent the legally protected opinions of the author and are presented for informational purposes only. Anyone who uses any of the information in the book does so at their own risk with the understanding that the author cannot be held responsible for the consequences. This document contains material protected under copyright laws. Any unauthorized reprint, transmission or resale of this material without the express permission of the author is strictly prohibited.

FTC Disclaimer: The author has no connection to nor was paid by any brand or product described in this document with the exception of any other books mentioned which were written by the author or published by Winter Tempest Books.

Printed in Great Britain
by Amazon

55318208R00083